WORKLESS SOCIETY

Expansion of the Leisure Class

WORKLESS SOCIETY

Expansion of the Leisure Class

V K Narayanan
Drexel University, USA

World Scientific

NEW JERSEY • LONDON • SINGAPORE • BEIJING • SHANGHAI • HONG KONG • TAIPEI • CHENNAI • TOKYO

Published by

World Scientific Publishing Co. Pte. Ltd.

5 Toh Tuck Link, Singapore 596224

USA office: 27 Warren Street, Suite 401-402, Hackensack, NJ 07601

UK office: 57 Shelton Street, Covent Garden, London WC2H 9HE

Library of Congress Cataloging-in-Publication Data
Names: Narayanan, V. K. (Veekay) author
Title: Workless society : expansion of the leisure class / V.K. Narayanan, Drexel University, USA.
Description: New Jersey : World Scientific Publishing, [2026] |
Includes bibliographical references and index.
Identifiers: LCCN 2026006156 | ISBN 9789819827749 hardcover |
ISBN 9789819827756 ebook | ISBN 9789819827763 ebook other
Subjects: LCSH: Leisure | Work
Classification: LCC HD4904.6 .N37 2026 | DDC 306.3/6--dc23/eng/20260306
LC record available at https://lccn.loc.gov/2026006156

British Library Cataloguing-in-Publication Data
A catalogue record for this book is available from the British Library.

For any available supplementary material, please visit
https://www.worldscientific.com/worldscibooks/10.1142/14717#t=suppl

Desk Editors: Aanand Jayaraman/Venkatesh Sandhya

Typeset by Stallion Press
Email: enquiries@stallionpress.com

Preface

The origins of this book can be traced to an invited talk I gave to a group of students in New Delhi, India, enrolled in the Fostiima MBA program crafted by my batchmates from the Indian Institute of Management, Ahmedabad. The year was 2020, and I had agreed to talk about technology change on Zoom from Princeton, NJ, in the midst of the COVID-19 pandemic. I had then used the term 'fifth wave' — borrowing the concept from Toffler, a giant in the field of futurism during the 70s. In that talk, I had made the bold prediction that in the not-too-distant future, a fifth wave of technology change will take place, ushered in by the onslaught of automation.

I was wrong in many details, especially about the speed of change, and in more ways than I can document in this preface.

If the invited talk began to crystallize some of the thoughts swirling in my head, the impetus to write a book came from another talk, this one I attended at Drexel University sometime later in 2020. The author of the talk, who will remain anonymous in this preface, had used sophisticated econometric analyses of their data about shifts in job categories from 1950 to 2000, to confidently predict that only repetitive jobs will be replaced by automation. In other words, managers and extension MBA students are safe from technological displacement. This flatly conflicted with the aims and projects run by my colleagues in the engineering school, some of which I had been aware of. By 2023, it had become clear to some, such as Eric Schmidt or the late Henry Kissinger, that Artificial Intelligence (AI) researchers may have unleashed a type of change difficult to control, with enormous consequences for existing political structures. My mind seems to agree with them: The genie is out of the bottle.

Initially, Veblen's 'leisure class' concept provided much of the conceptual fuel for my thoughts, but as I proceeded, I saw the potential of change beyond the expansion of the leisure class, in the early formulation of the ideas of this book. It was around this time that Lucassen's magisterial book on work appeared, and I reformulated earlier ideas into the concept of a workless society.

As I note in the final chapter, the workless society does *not* exist as of now, but the concept provides a debating platform for many different perspectives. I believe that the concept enables us to escape the sterile dichotomy of capitalism and communism. When I recently shared my thoughts via a paper at the Philosophy of Management Conference in the UK, I witnessed an interesting phenomenon: The Marxist-oriented elder scholars resented the idea, but the younger academics, perhaps below the age of 40, found it easy to grasp (and cheer) the potential of emerging technology.

As a doctoral student, caught up in the excitement of the organization development field that flourished in the 1970s, I have been interested in the design of work that emancipated human beings from the tyranny of their workplace. Hence, it took only a short leap of imagination to move to the concept of a workless society, which releases individuals from engaging in activities in which they do not find meaning, activities that could be relegated to relevant technological tools and methods.

Finally, I would like to thank numerous individuals in this endeavor. First, Liam Fahey, Nicholas O'Reagan, and Rich Wokutch, all of whom enthusiastically supported my book proposal. Second, Suri Lee, the talented doctoral student in strategy at LeBow, contributed enormously through her research assistance. Needless to say, I owe an enormous debt of gratitude to the World Scientific's editor, Rochelle Kronzek, for her sponsorship and her staff for their diligent work.

This book is intended to stir debate, not offer a packaged solution. The ultimate beneficiaries of such debate are likely to be the younger generations: Generations Z, Alpha, and Beta. I dedicate this book to my grandson Ando Raymolnd Costillo Narayanan, whose generation (Beta), I hope, will take humanity to a better place beyond our imagination.

About the Author

V.K. Narayanan is the Deloitte & Touché Jones Stubbs Professor of Strategy and Entrepreneurship at Drexel University. He was the founding Associate Dean for research in LeBow College of Business. Formerly, he had served as the Director of the Center for Management of Technology and the Associate Dean for Academic Affairs in the School of Business at the University of Kansas. He had also been a recipient of the Fulbright-Nehru Senior Faculty Fellow, Fulbright-FLAD Chair in Management of Technology at the University of Aveiro, Koch Industries Fellowship (1994–1996), and Phillips Petroleum Fellowship (1984–1987). In 2019, he was recognized with the Albert Nelson Marquis Lifetime Achievement Award by Marquis *Who's Who*. Narayanan had served as a member of the Academic Advisory Board of Project Management Institute and has published five books and monographs as well as cited papers in major business journals in a number of disciplines. SSCI ranks him among the top ten researchers in the management of technology and the top 150 researchers in strategy. Narayanan holds a bachelor's degree in mechanical engineering from the Indian Institute of Technology, Madras, a postgraduate degree in business administration from the Indian Institute of Management, Ahmedabad, and a PhD in business from the Graduate School of Business at the University of Pittsburgh,

Pennsylvania. He has had behavioral training with the *National Training Laboratories*, Bethel, Maine, of which he is currently a member. Narayanan has been a consultant to large pharmaceutical and high technology companies primarily in strategy implementation and corporate innovation.

Contents

Chapter 1

Introduction

Abstract

The concept of work has been analyzed from a diverse set of perspectives, but almost all analyses adopt an instrumental view of work: They primarily discuss what functions are performed by work. However, when work is viewed as a set of activities, it is easily seen that the nature of work has changed considerably. Because we hold on to the assumption that work is inevitable, the ubiquity of work as an assumption lies underneath all of our analyses. Given the technological developments in the last two decades, I introduce the idea that we may have come to a point in our civilization where a workless society is possible.

Work: What is it? Why do we do it? Can we do without it? Such questions related to the concept of work are nowadays rarely discussed or, at worst, dismissed as not worthy of attention. And yet, the actuality of work is evident to everyone: Most of us spend a significant share of our waking life working in organizations. We earn wages to support our families, make our friends, and sometimes even find our spouses in the organizations we work for. Most often, we take work for granted so that it has now become a background assumption.

Because work is ubiquitous, our conception of work pervades our family structures, the design of organizations, and even policy decisions. For example, in the US at least, our family structures have evolved from predominantly nuclear to include two-career families. COVID-19 punctured a hole in our belief that we need to go to the workplace, work needs to be done there, and there only. Every election cycle, we hear a debate about minimum wage and other job-related matters — all of which assume the inevitability of work. Rarely do we sit back and question if all of this is necessary.

In the meantime, technological advances have reshaped our world, including the world of work. Most of us simply don't do at work what our immediate ancestors — parents or grandparents — did. The impending technological advances have raised angst and optimism, and some eager enthusiasts have even started to argue for the end of work as we know it. It is time we examine the ubiquity of work as an assumption woven into the fabric of our lives.

In this book I invite you to peer under our beliefs about work.

The Concept of Work: A Variety of Views

Historically, the concept of work has been of interest to many individuals with different persuasions, not merely to economists and management theorists.[1] They range from religious scholars to labor union leaders. A brisk walk over history will alert us to the wide variety of meanings associated with work.

Religion[2]: Some religious texts view work as a punishment. God had created a world in which Adam and Eve had "dominion over the fish of the sea, and over the birds of the air, and over the cattle, and over all the wild animals of the earth" (Genesis, 1:26). Moreover, they were granted to "freely eat of every tree of the garden; but of the tree of the knowledge of good and evil" (Genesis, 2:15). Life in the Garden of Eden thus appeared to be workless. When Adam and Eve committed the original sin, God cursed them "among all animals and among all wild creatures" (Genesis, 3:14). Adam was condemned to cultivate "by the sweat of (his) face"

---

[1]For an etymological treatment of the word, work, please refer to: https://yoannbazin.com/2014/10/08/untangling-work-an-etymological-exploration/#:~:text=A%20noble%20linguistic%20trail:%20%CE%B5%CF%81%CE%B3%CE%BF%CE%BD,noble%20realization%20of%20human%20activities.

[2]In looking for the origin of words, simply tracing their form is not the end. Once these trails are followed, the meaning of words is anchored in their socio-historical context. In the case of work, Judaeo-Christianity has deeply influenced how social work practices were considered in society. Through its mythology, the Ancient Testament heavily anchors the idea of work.

(Genesis, 3:17) the ground that was then cursed. Consequently, for Adam, being cast away from the Garden of Eden was the beginning of the need for work.

But an entirely different theme is also propagated by many religious scholars. They have proposed that "work is worship," meaning that dedicated work can be a form of spiritual service. The idea of "work is worship" has roots in various religious and philosophical traditions, including Christianity, Hinduism, and Islam. The Bible, particularly Colossians 3:23–24, encourages working heartily for the Lord, emphasizing that our work is a form of service to Christ. In Hinduism, the concept of Karma Yoga is often taken to mean that selfless action or work done for the welfare of humanity is a path to spiritual growth. The Hebrew word "avodah" can mean both "work" and "worship" or "service" in the Old Testament, suggesting that work can be a form of worship. In Islam, work is considered an act of worship, provided certain criteria are met.

Psychology: Psychologist Freud[3] is credited with saying that the two things a person in good mental health should be able to do well are "to love and to work" ("lieben und arbeiten"). Freud's biographers note that Freud was not wealthy, independently or dependently, but because he was in love with Martha Bernays, Freud knew he had to find a way to earn a respectable income before he could marry Martha. Thus, he chose to go into private practice, for the money, but he made neurology his specialty to pursue his real interest. His work was creative, prodigious, and groundbreaking; even if much of it has not stood the test of time, it spurred much of what has proved useful in modern psychology. And by all accounts, Freud remained engrossed in his work until his death, just as he remained close to his wife and six children. Although there is no direct evidence for the attribution of "Leiben und arbieiten," to Freud, it is quite believable that he would point to love and to work as the hallmark of a mentally healthy individual.

[3]Sigmund Freud (1856–1939) was the founder of psychoanalysis, a clinical method for evaluating and treating pathologies seen as originating from conflicts in the psyche, through dialogue between patient and psychoanalyst, and the distinctive theory of mind and human agency derived from it. In founding psychoanalysis, Freud developed therapeutic techniques such as the use of free association and discovered transference, establishing its central role in the analytic process. Though in decline as a diagnostic and clinical practice, psychoanalysis remains influential within psychology, psychiatry, psychotherapy, and across the humanities.

Later psychologists would consider "work" as a "multifaceted" domain that explores the relationship between individuals and their work environment, including its impact on well-being, behavior, and overall satisfaction. For example, vocational psychologists address issues like job dissatisfaction, career transitions, and the impact of unemployment; industrial organization (IO) psychologists aim to create a positive and productive work environment that fosters employee satisfaction and engagement. Psychologists recognize that work is not just a means of livelihood; it's also a source of identity, social connection, and personal fulfillment.

Economics: Economists have had a strong interest in the labor market, and macroeconomists have been interested in national-level unemployment rates. Indeed, unemployment rates feature in many policy-level decisions, especially the Federal Reserve's decision to modify interest rates. No enumeration of work in economics could ignore the differences in economic views of Adam Smith and Karl Marx, two thinkers[4] who, though not contemporaries, have ignited a lot of debates about work in our public policy (Spencer, 2024). For Adam Smith, society would have to endure less meaningful work in order to improve efficiency. With his analysis of the division of labor, Adam argued that this cost was the price of higher economic growth. Marx, unlike Smith, stressed the class origins of worker resistance and linked workers' alienating experience of work to the extraction of surplus value in work. He also argued — again, unlike Smith — that meaningful work could be achieved.

In addition to the diversity of conceptions in various branches of learning, there are also very specific ideas about the functions and consequences, of work.

---

[4] Adam Smith was an 18th-century Scottish philosopher, economist, and author, considered the father of modern economics. He is best known for his 1776 book, *An Inquiry into the Nature and Causes of the Wealth of Nations*, often cited as the beginning of both economics and capitalism. This book laid the foundation for classical free market economic theory. It argued that free trade, open markets, and competition would lead to greater prosperity than stringent government regulations. Karl Marx (German: was a German philosopher, political theorist, and an economist. He is best-known for the pamphlet *The Communist Manifesto* (written with Friedrich Engels), and his three-volume *Das Kapital* (1867–1894), a critique of classical political economy. Marx's ideas and their subsequent development, collectively known as Marxism, have had enormous influence.

Work as a source of meaning: For many, work is a source of meaning. There is a story about John F. Kennedy, the 35th President of the United States.[5] In 1962, President John F. Kennedy visited the National Aeronautics and Space Administration (NASA), and during his tour of the facility, he met a janitor who was carrying a broom down the hallway. The President then casually asked the janitor what he did for NASA, and the janitor replied, "I'm helping put a man on the moon." It is said that the janitor kept the building clean so that the scientists, engineers, and astronauts could focus on their mission of putting "man on the moon". They did not have to worry about spending their time on trash cans, bathrooms, or hallways. The janitor tied his purpose with theirs.

Work as a source of identity: For some work is a source of identity. For many Americans, work provides a sense of purpose, accomplishment, and identity. Professional achievements are often seen as a validation of one's skills, intelligence, and worth. Thus, work is a foundation of Americans' identity, the core of our self-image. We are what we do. The overall trend toward secularization has diminished religion's role as the primary source of identity, and professional success has taken precedence in public and social life. It is also noted that this identification has come with some costs. For example, identifying too strongly with work can lead to feelings of self-worth tied to career achievements, making setbacks or job loss feel like a personal failure. The focus on work can lead to neglecting family, friends, or other hobbies. Additionally, job loss can lead to feelings of isolation and a loss of social support. When work becomes a primary source of identity, it can be challenging to maintain a healthy work–life balance. This can lead to workaholism, where work is prioritized over other important aspects of life.

Work as a source of community: The concept of work as a community emphasizes the social and relational aspects of employment. In this view, workplaces are social organizations where people connect, collaborate, and contribute to shared goals. It focuses on fostering a sense of belonging, trust, and mutual support among employees. The social connections are deemed to be crucial for well-being, engagement, and organizational success.

---

[5]https://fromthegreennotebook.com/2017/11/04/the-janitor-who-help-put-a-man-on-the-moon/.

Work as a source of status: Work often defines an individual's status both inside and outside the organization she works for. "Status" refers to social standing, respect, and prominence within their work group. It reflects how others perceive their influence, importance, and reputation within the company. The level of respect and recognition an individual receives from others is often linked to their skills, experience, or contributions. In essence, status is a combination of how an employee is perceived and how they act in their role, shaping their interactions and influence within the organization.

The views touched upon above are widely different, but they all adopt an *instrumental* view of work. Through an instrumentalist lens, work is a "mere means," to borrow Kant's[6] terminology. To view work instrumentally is to value work only insofar as it furthers some external end, rather than as an end in itself. In religion, it is a source of punishment or worship; in psychology, it is one avenue to satisfaction; in economics, it is meant for efficient production or exploitation. Alternatively, work could give meaning, a sense of identity, provide community, and status. Few of the views peer inside the black box of "work" that provides the means to the end they are interested in.

In contrast, an activity-based view poses the questions: What is work? What does it constitute? The answers to these questions have been changing over the years. We have known for a long time that our work activities have been changing over the years.

Changing Nature of Work

As human civilization has progressed, what we do as work in our daily lives has changed significantly. Let us examine a few examples:

[6]Immanuel Kant (1724–12 February 1804) was a German philosopher and one of the central Enlightenment thinkers. Kant's works in epistemology, metaphysics, ethics, and aesthetics have made him one of the most influential and highly discussed figures in modern moral philosophy, in which the concept of using someone "merely as a means" refers to treating them solely as a tool to achieve one's own ends, without recognizing their intrinsic worth or autonomy. It violates the fundamental principle of the Formula of Humanity, which states that we should always treat humanity in ourselves and others as an end in itself, and never merely as a means.

Agriculture: A hundred years ago, farmers grew crops and raised livestock primarily for their own consumption, with little or no sale of produce. Their work was largely *manual*, utilizing horse-drawn plows and hand tools for tasks like planting, cultivating, and harvesting. Their activities included plowing, planting, cultivating (they cultivated by hand or with horse-drawn cultivators to remove weeds), and harvesting. They also took care of animal care and farm maintenance. A farmer's job has drastically changed in the past 100 years, transitioning from primarily manual labor with animal-powered tools to modern, technology-driven farming practices. Today, farmers utilize tractors, harvesters, and other machinery for efficient cultivation, planting, and harvesting. It should not be surprising that, according to data from the Farm Labor Survey (FLS) of the USDA's National Agricultural Statistical Service (NASS),[7] the number of self-employed and family farm workers declined from 7.60 million in 1950 to 2.01 million in 1990, a 74% reduction.[8]

Industry: Over the last 100 years, traditional factory work has shifted to more skilled and automated work. Technological advancements, including robotics and computer-aided manufacturing, have led to increased automation in industrial processes, reducing the need for human labor in certain areas. The shift from manual labor to high-tech manufacturing has dramatically altered the nature of industrial work. Partly as a result, the percentage of the workforce employed in manufacturing has declined significantly, while the service sector has grown substantially. It is also true that international trade and outsourcing have resulted in the relocation of some industrial jobs to countries with lower labor costs. Also, industrial jobs have become more specialized and require higher levels of education and training, as technology has advanced.

Finance: Over the last 100 years, finance jobs have also evolved significantly, due to several forces. For one, technology has automated many traditional tasks, leading to increased efficiency in finance teams. Second,

---

[7]The USDA's (United States Department of Agriculture) National Agricultural Statistics Service (NASS) conducts hundreds of surveys every year and prepares reports covering virtually every aspect of US agriculture.

[8]https://www.ers.usda.gov/topics/farm-economy/farm-labor#:~:text=More%20Farmworkers%20Are%20Settled%2C%20Fewer%20Are%20Migrants&text=This%20share%20is%20up%20from,the%20United%20States%20since%202007.

the emergence of fintech companies has further disrupted the industry, offered innovative solutions, and created new job roles focused on technology and data analysis. Third, the rise of the Internet and mobile banking has transformed how people interact with financial institutions, creating new job opportunities in areas like cybersecurity and digital marketing. Fourth, the industry has expanded its focus from the original banking and loan operations to encompass a broader range of activities, including asset management, investment banking, and financial technology. This has led to both a shift in the types of skills required and[9] the types of roles available within the sector. Overall employment in business and financial occupations is projected to grow faster than the average for all occupations from 2023 to 2033.[10]

Writing: Over the past century, the writing job has also undergone a dramatic transformation, influenced by technological advancements and evolving societal needs. Earlier, the job consisted of newspaper reporters and novelists, but today it also includes digital content creators and social media managers. The introduction of the typewriter revolutionized the writing process, allowing for faster and more efficient drafting and editing. The advent of computers and word processors further accelerated this, enabling writers to revise, edit, and collaborate more easily than ever before. The internet and social media platforms have created a sizable demand for online content, leading to new writing jobs like content marketing, blog writing, and social media management. From traditional novels and articles to blog posts, short-form videos, and interactive online experiences, the range of writing genres has expanded significantly. Writers today need to be adept at using a variety of digital tools and platforms, including content management systems, social media management tools, and editing software.

---

[9] https://www.google.com/search?q=change+in+finance++jobs+over+the+century&sca_esv=8775833c1dfface9&rlz=1C1GCEV_enUS991US992&biw=1280&bih=551&sxsrf=AHTn8zoxZ1u7qvVBRMAfQww56_lL5wm0jw%3A1744584918944&ei=1kD8Z-ysOaaf5NoPuMPtuAc&ved=0ahUKEwjs7_6ijdaMAxWmD1kFH.

[10] *ibid.*

Teaching and research: As the Khan Academy founder, Salman Khan[11] notes, in the 18th century, humans had the utopian idea of offering mass public education to everyone. Because resources were scarce, instead of being able to give every student a private tutor, we bunched them together in groups of 30 or so, and applied standard processes to them, in the form of lectures and periodic assessments. Khan (2024) would argue that with generative AI, increased personalization is possible, and with it, greater expectations from the teacher.

What is happening on the research front is even more intriguing. Let me cite three examples:

1. AI is transforming how we do research: In 2024, research published in journals like *Nature* found that elephants use specific sounds to identify each other, similar to how humans use names. This research, which suggests elephants may have a rudimentary form of language, with the ability to recognize and respond to specific vocalizations, involved analyzing elephant calls and using *machine learning.*[12]
2. Algorithmic management is pervading the practice of science: World Wide Web, Google Scholar, MTurk, and other online study platforms are now standard, and these were not available even two decades ago. Digitization first, and now, the generative AI is expected to transform what we do as researchers.
3. The constraints of space, having disappeared, new forms of publications appeared, including the open-access journals such as PLOS.[13]

As the aforementioned examples illustrate, what we do at work has changed over time, although many job titles and labels have remained the same. But the stability in job labels should not mislead us: We are doing different things now, compared to what we did even a decade ago.

---

[11] Salman "Sal" Amin Khan is an American educator and the founder of Khan Academy, a free online non-profit educational platform. He is an ardent advocate of the use of AI to improve education. He has elaborated his views on teaching in his book Brae New Word (2024). He is also the founder of Khan Lab School, a private in-person school in Mountain View, California. https://en.wikipedia.org/wiki/Sal_Khan.

[12] https://e360.yale.edu/digest/elephant-names-study.

[13] PLOS One (stylized PLOS ONE, and formerly PLoS ONE) is a peer-reviewed open access mega journal published by the Public Library of Science (PLOS) since 2006.

Indeed, in addition to job labels, we hold on to numerous assumptions about work. But first, what are assumptions and how do we unravel them?

Assumptions

Cambridge Dictionary defines assumption as something that "you accept as true without questions or proof." It is said to be derived from Latin assumptio, meaning "a taking or receiving," Although originally it had religious connotations, e.g., describing "the reception of the Virgin Mary into heaven," the word has shed its religious roots and developed into the noun we hear more often today. Just as fish take water for granted, humans take many beliefs to be true. These beliefs are labeled assumptions, usually when a person takes them for granted without much reflection.

Assumptions are a *double-edged* sword. They allow us to process information and make decisions quickly, which is essential for navigating daily life; they can be a starting point for exploring new ideas and forming hypotheses, and in some cases, they can also be a helpful way to make choices when complete information is unavailable. But assumptions can lead to misunderstandings in relationships and communication; can perpetuate stereotypes and biases, leading to unfair treatment and discrimination; relying on assumptions without verification can result in poor decisions and negative outcomes; they can limit our ability to think outside the box and explore new possibilities.

Assumptions vary according to their *depth*. Surface assumptions are invoked explicitly for developing an argument or a point of view, but participants in the discussion are aware and can explicitly state them. Witness the axioms underpinning Euclid's geometry: even advanced practitioners of geometry — who may have internalized these assumptions — can reel off these assumptions. Deeper assumptions are shared and quite often tacit. Other individuals in the community hold the same or similar assumptions. Due to reasons of communicative efficiency, individuals do not have to talk explicitly about them. And these assumptions may have gone beneath their awareness. In other words, these assumptions become tacit.

Quite often these assumptions *insidiously* influence human reasoning. Deeper assumptions are often undiscussed and undiscussable (Argyris, 1977) if there are cultural taboos that preclude open articulation of the assumption. This is perhaps succinctly captured by the modern British philosopher, T. E. Hulme (Thomson, 1962):

> There are certain doctrines which for a particular period seem not doctrines, but inevitable categories of the human mind. Men do not look at them merely as correct opinions, for they have become so much part of the mind, and lie so far back, that they are never really conscious of them at all. It is these abstract ideas at the center, things which they take for granted that characterize a period.[14]

Assumptions influence our thinking and discourse in at least three ways. First, they *restrict* the scope of issues available for discussion. For example, no one felt the need to question the geocentric theory of the world: It was self-evident, a belief maintained by the culture. Second, it restricted the options that are available to a decision maker. Flat-earth theorists could not conceive of the sea route charted by Columbus.[15] Third, it influences the causal logic that pervades our justification for action. Eugenics allowed its believers to propose selective breeding until it was debunked.

Tools for Assumption Analysis

Because of their importance, several approaches have been crafted to identify and analyze assumptions. The following are a few examples:

1. *Formal analysis* of assumptions involves systematically identifying, stating, and evaluating assumptions, particularly in fields like formal verification, statistics, and research. This process helps ensure that assumptions are clearly defined and that their potential impact is understood, leading to more reliable and accurate results.

---

[14] Quoted in Thomson (1962) and Hulme (1994).

[15] Christopher Columbus is famous for his 1492 voyage across the Atlantic Ocean, which he believed would lead to Asia, but instead brought him to the Americas. This voyage is considered the beginning of European exploration and colonization of the Americas and is also linked to the Columbian Exchange.

2. *Scenario planning* involves creating and analyzing different potential futures based on varying assumptions to prepare for uncertainties. It's not about predicting the future, but about exploring how different sets of assumptions could impact a business or project. By identifying and testing these scenarios, organizations can develop more robust strategies and decision-making processes.
3. *Philosophical analysis*, examining assumptions, involves identifying the presuppositions or *unstated* beliefs underlying a statement or argument. The assumptions could be ontological (which relates to the nature of reality, what exists and what does not), epistemological (focusing on how knowledge is acquired, what constitutes knowledge, and how it can be justified), axiological (involving values and ethics), methodological (concerning the methods and procedures used to study or analyze a particular topic), or rhetorical (how a philosophical argument is presented and evaluated). Assumption analysis is crucial for understanding the validity and potential limitations of philosophical claims, as well as for identifying potential inconsistencies or misunderstandings.
4. *Science fiction*, where researchers have posited that exposure to imaginative narratives and depictions of futuristic technologies may stimulate creative thinking by encouraging individuals to consider novel ideas and question conventional assumptions (Vorderer *et al.*, 2004).

In this book, I do not use any formal tools of analysis. Instead, similar to what is found in an exercise in philosophical analysis, I juxtapose two streams of thought. The first stream is about technological change. We know that the last two decades have witnessed significant technological change; this change has been accelerating and transforming our lives. The second related stream is the impact of technological change on organizations and the nature of work. One potential outcome of linking the two streams of thought is an inescapable conclusion that work as we know it may be unnecessary. Although I am not alone in arriving at this conclusion,[16] the assumption of worklessness has not yet received a fair hearing.

[16]Some authors have recently alluded to the possibility of workless societies, e.g., Kissinger *et al.* (2024). Similarly, techno entrepreneurs like Elon Musk have also discussed the possibility.

Before we get too far ahead, let me clarify my choice of the term "worklessness." Specifically, I want to distinguish unemployment, a term we are all familiar with, from "worklessness," a term I use here in this book. "Unemployed" means not having a paid job, not being employed. A person who's described as unemployed is typically out of work and looking for a job. A person who's retired, for example, wouldn't be said to be unemployed. Economists refer to unemployment as a situation where individuals who are able and willing to work are unable to find employment. It's measured by the unemployment rate, which is the percentage of the labor force that is unemployed. These are important concepts, but worklessness is a state where individuals do *not* have to work. They may engage in several activities of their own volition, but are not interested in the transactional nature of work where they get paid. In many societies, a select group of individuals, an elite, have enjoyed the benefit of worklessness. The assumption of ubiquity of work refers not to a select group of individuals, but to society as a whole.

The Assumption of Ubiquity of Work

It is a reasonable assumption that most of us will have to work. We may derive our identity from the workplace, we may find meaning in work, we may get to the workplace for engagement or community, and of course, we will work to earn money to support our lives. Work *is* ubiquitous, and most treatises on work do not find it necessary to justify the assumption of the ubiquity of work.

This book is about work, but more precisely about *worklessness*.

Although there is not much evidence for worklessness, I will argue that from a work-as-activity lens, we may have come to a point in the evolution of our civilization — thanks to technological developments — where the *possibility*, not the probability, of worklessness can be contemplated. A workless society is not inevitable,[17] but a negation of the ubiquity of work challenges some of our actions and policies while at the same time opening up overlooked options.

Although the idea of "worklessness" has not to any great extent occupied either scholarly or popular interest, a related idea — leisure — has

[17]Thus, this book does not adopt a technological determinist position, taken by champions of AI like Elon Musk.

been discussed by some. Interest in leisure as a topic of scholarly interest was triggered by Thorstein Veblen's *Theory of the Leisure Class*. We could get some insights into a workless society through an understanding of leisure. In other words, leisure could be a metaphor for worklessness. To be sure, worklessness is not the same as leisure,[18] and the activities in which Veblen's leisure class was immersed may be vastly different from the activities of humans in a workless society.

The purpose of the book is to put forth the assumption of worklessness, in contrast to the ubiquity of work that has undergirded most of our conversations about work. As noted earlier in this chapter, work can be viewed as a set of activities, and this perspective is distinct from the instrumental views of work that have been prevalent in scholarship. This perspective helps me elaborate on the idea of workless societies. I will develop the idea in the following steps:

1. Work, as we know it today, is a byproduct of the industrial society that has been the dominant social form in developed nations during the 20th century.
2. The activities that comprise work have been changing over the years, mostly because of technological change.
3. After the advent of industrial societies, automation, a central logic behind major technological change, has displaced human activity with technology.
4. The early phases of automation, primarily robotics, have eviscerated repetitive activities in organizations. That is, humans do not need to engage in repetitive tasks such as the ones found in assembly line factories of yore.
5. More recent advances in Artificial Intelligence (AI) are making it possible to automate not merely computing, but the reasoning process as well.
6. Thus, the concept of worklessness is *possible*, but its prevalence is restrained by our enduring assumption of scarcity and our need for control. But workless societies have their own challenges: they may

[18]Thorstein Veblen, who elaborated on the leisure class, has been a source of inspiration for this manuscript, but he was writing in the Gilded Age, he did not take a work as activity lens. And he had also presented a basis of differentiation in society, something this manuscript goes not attempt to do.

bring in festering social, psychological, and sociological problems to the forefront.
7. Worklessness is an option that needs to occupy us and our policymakers.

In what follows, I provide a chapter-by-chapter roadmap for the book.

In the following chapter, I revisit Thorstein Veblen's classic on the theory of the leisure class. Because the ubiquity of work has been such a pervasive assumption, there has been limited consideration of worklessness. An exception is the leisure class concept advanced by Thorstein Veblen. However, the Gilded Age during which Veblen was writing has been transformed by over a century of technological progress, and we can now visualize a society where the purely work-based distinction between elite and commoner is obsolete. I owe an intellectual debt to Veblen for identifying several characteristics of work, which I will parlay into developing the concept of worklessness.

In the third chapter, I demonstrate that there have been diverse conceptualizations of work over the years. I do this in three ways. First, I summarize Lucassen's historical model, which narrates the history of work from prehistoric days to the modern industrial age. The model clearly demonstrates that work as we know it today is a recent concept, a product of the industrial age. Second, in the 20th century, a managerialist perspective that arose first in the US and then in Europe put forth the idea that work can be designed for organizational efficiency and human satisfaction. The designers focused on work activities, the social system of work, and the context of work. Third, in the second half of the 20th century, futurists like Toffler pointed out the changing nature of work as a result of information technology.

In the fourth chapter, I provide a sweeping overview of the contributions of economists to our understanding of work. For one, more than any other discipline, economists understand that technology plays a central role in what we consider work. They also provided the concept of long waves to capture the long-term consequences of major technology innovations. Economists perceptively saw that technology both destroyed and created new tasks and were among the first to document quantitatively the effect of technology on unemployment.

In the fifth and sixth chapters, I lay out the effects of automation on work. Indeed, the chapters summarize the story of automation-related technological change during the second half of the 20th century. In the fifth chapter, I focus on robotics and digitization. The first phase of automation, robotics, replaced manual repetitive activities with technology. Robotics embraced numerous technologies and affected a whole lot of industries. The effects of roboticization were felt mainly on the shop floor, and modern-day factories have few laborers on the shop floor. The early phase of digitalization consisted of the introduction of Information and computing technologies (ICT) in organizations, which impacted mostly clerical and word processing activities. The later phases, which consisted of moving from analog to digital regimes, enabled new data that could be brought under the control of automation.

In the sixth chapter, I continue the story of automation, specifically on AI. AI is believed to be capable of automating reasoning processes. Although this is a story in progress, the possibility of a workerless society has increased with the developments in AI.

In the seventh chapter, I set forth the main argument of the book: we have been captured by the tacit assumption that work is ubiquitous, overlooking the possibility that work may not be necessary. We have narrowed the meaning of work to a set of activities that we as employees do in industrial settings. Technological change obviates the need for most of these activities. Automation has obviated the need for repetitive tasks or what Talcott Parsons characterized as the technical level of an organization. Advances in digitalization are making it possible to automate managerial work. We continue to overlook the possibility that work as currently conceived may not be necessary.

In the eighth chapter, I address the dark side of workless societies. First, I enumerate the two fundamental barriers to the acceptance of the workless society assumption: the scarcity mindset and the need for control. Second, a workless society, where non-work is the norm, is likely to face significant challenges arising from the release of time from work.

In the ninth chapter, to illustrate the idea that a workless society remains an unexamined assumption, I enumerate three policy changes proposed in the US, policies relating to changes in minimum wage, health care, and Universal Basic Income. I note that all three proposals are undergirded by a scarcity mindset but with slightly different orientations to social control. With the exception of a variant of UBI, none of these proposals displays any awareness of the impending changes wrought by technology development.

In the tenth chapter, I lay out three potential misconceptions about a workless society and outline a set of issues that we collectively should examine for the future. As AI is moving the concept of a workless society from being a figment of imagination to reality, our governance structures are lagging. We are at a generative moment when we need to fashion a society to our will.

A note to the readers: As can be seen from the aforementioned contents of each chapter, most readers will benefit from reading the chapters in sequence to glean the cluster of evidence and ideas that hold together the assumption of a workless society. To those who are steeped in scholarship, who may find some early chapters covering familiar terrain, I suggest that you focus on the core argument of the book laid out in Chapters 7 and 8. To those who are quick to embrace the concept of a workless society, I would encourage you to also consider the challenges ahead (Chapter 8). At the moment, a workless society is an assumption, and we have work to do.

Silicon Valley has been a notable breeding ground for disruptive technologies such as AI that lie at the base of a workless society. While the entrepreneurs of the valley may be driven by a desire to create products and services, thereby creating value, a workless society offers the potential for releasing humans from mundane activities that they have to carry out to navigate their daily lives. It is a possibility we should grasp, the earlier the better.

References

Argyris, C. (1977). Double loop learning in organizations. *Harvard Business Review*, 55(5), 115–125.

Hulme, T. E. (1994). *The Collected Writings of TE Hulme*.

Khan, S. (2024). *Brave New Words: How AI Will Revolutionize Education (and why That's a Good Thing)*. New York: Penguin, p. 12.

Spencer, D. (2024). Efficiency vs. meaningful work: A critical survey of historical and contemporary debates, *Contributions to Political Economy*, Volume 43(1), 21–36. https://doi.org/10.1093/cpe/bzae009.

Thomson, D. (1962). *Europe Since Napoleon*, p. 655. *(No Title)*. See also Hulme, T. E. (1994). *The Collected Writings of TE Hulme*.

Vorderer, P., Klimmt, C., and Ritterfeld, U. (2004). Enjoyment: At the heart of media entertainment. *Communication Theory*, 14(4), 388–408.

Chapter 2

Leisure Class Revisited

Abstract

This chapter opens a discussion of the central possibility that technological developments in the making have the potential to create a workless society. I revisit an old classic, *The Theory of the Leisure Class: An Economic Study in the Evolution of Social Institutions*, by the academic, Thorstein Veblen, first to introduce the idea that the age in which he lived, has been drastically transformed by technological developments in the 20th century, an idea that will be elaborated in the next chapter, secondly to advance the idea that whereas Veblen conceptualized the leisure class as an elite, we can now visualize a society where the distinction between the elite and commoner purely based on work is obsolete, and thirdly, and almost by implication, to offer homage to an intellect that has stimulated the thinking behind this book.

In the United States, the period from about the late 1870s to the late 1890s — the period that occurred between the Reconstruction Era and the Progressive Era[1] – had by the 1920s, begun to be referred to as the Gilded Age. Although historians may continue to debate the exact beginning and ending of the Gilded Age, for our purpose, we will simply stick with what most can agree on: the Gilded Age was a time of rapid

[1]Reconstruction Era and the Progressive Era — Two major reform periods in the US history: one addressing post-Civil War racial and political integration (1865–1877), and the other targeting industrial reform, labor rights, and democratic expansion (1890s–1920s).

economic growth. During this period, the US took over the industrial leadership from Britain, rapidly expanding its economy in factories, railroads, and coal mining. Investors in London and Paris poured money into the railroads through the American financial market centered on Wall Street. It was also a time for monopolies in the US, the most famous being Standard Oil.[2] These monopolies also signaled the spiraling economic inequality in society.

The term, Gilded Age was borrowed from one of Mark Twain's[3] not-so-prominent novels, *The Gilded Age: A Tale of Today* (1873). Twain used the novel to demonstrate how the great wealth of the few at the top of society contrasted with the poor living and working conditions of the many. Indeed, the Gilded Age witnessed the emergence of the super-rich — Vanderbilts, Morgans, and Goulds,[4] to name just three. But the age was simultaneously a period of extreme *economic inequality*. For example, one estimate suggests that from 1860 to 1900, the wealthiest 2% of American households owned more than a third of the nation' s wealth, while the top 10% owned roughly three-quarters of it. The bottom 40% had no wealth at all. In terms of property, the wealthiest 1% owned 51%, while the bottom 44% claimed 1.1%. In comparison, in 2024, the top 10% of households held 67% of total household wealth, whereas the bottom 50% of households held only 2.5% of total household wealth.[5] The Gilded Age proved to be the target of trenchant criticism by numerous public intellectuals, and one of those, Thorstein Veblen focused his attention on income inequality.

---

[2]Founded by John D. Rockefeller in 1870, Standard Oil grew to dominate the American oil industry and became a symbol of monopolistic capitalism. Its dissolution in 1911 under antitrust law was a landmark in US corporate regulation.

[3]Mark Twain, the pen name of Samuel Langhorne Clemens, was one of America's most influential writers and satirists. Best known for *The Adventures of Tom Sawyer* (1876) and *Adventures of Huckleberry Finn* (1885), Twain captured the spirit, contradictions, and injustices of 19th-century American life. His work offers sharp critiques of slavery, social hypocrisy, and industrial greed.

[4]Vanderbilts, Morgans, and Goulds to name just three. Cornelius Vanderbilt (railroads), JP Morgan (finance), and Jay Gould (railroads/speculation) were key figures of the Gilded Age who amassed great fortunes and exerted significant influence over American industrial development. They are often cited as "robber barons" due to their aggressive business tactics.

[5]https://www.statista.com/statistics/220093/number-of-billionaires-in-the-united-states/#:~:text=In%202023%2C%20there%20were%20around,globally%202024%2C%20by%20net%20worth.

Thorstein Veblen's Leisure Class

Thorstein Bunde Veblen was an American economist and sociologist, perhaps best known for his book, *The Theory of the Leisure Class* (1899). He advanced the concept of the leisure class, a social group characterized by several interrelated features that distinguish it from other classes, particularly those engaged in productive or industrial labor. His *Theory of Leisure Class* presented the then novel concepts of *conspicuous consumption* and *conspicuous leisure*, and the book laid the foundation for a perspective on institutional economics in which Veblen pioneered the idea that an economy is significantly embedded in social institutions.

Veblen erected his societal analysis on the distinction between the leisure and non-leisure classes.[6] Being the elite, the leisure class enjoys status, power, and prestige, and the distinction between the leisure and non-leisure classes hinges on lifestyle choices that are deeply embedded in society's social and economic structures. We reproduce six key characteristics of the leisure class:

1. *Exemption from productive labor*: A fundamental characteristic of the leisure class is its exemption from productivity, especially manual labor. This exemption is a status symbol, signifying that the individual or family has sufficient wealth and social standing not to need to engage in labor for subsistence. This disdain for productive work is rooted in a historical association of manual labor with servitude or lower status.
2. *Vicarious leisure and conspicuous consumption*: The leisure class demonstrates its status through vicarious leisure — leisure enjoyed indirectly through the labor of others, such as servants — and conspicuous consumption. Vicarious leisure manifests in the employment of individuals whose primary roles are to perform the productive tasks and household duties that the leisure class members avoid. Conspicuous consumption involves spending on goods and services that are not necessary for comfort or survival but are indicators of wealth and leisure. This consumption includes tangible goods, services, and leisure activities that display the owner's ability to afford a lifestyle beyond productive labor.

[6] I am grateful to Lee, Seungju for an initial draft summary of Veblen, which has since been edited.

3. *Predatory origins and pecuniary emulation*: The leisure class's origins in predatory culture contribute to its *competitive* nature, particularly regarding wealth accumulation and display. This competitive ethos manifests as pecuniary emulation, where members of the leisure class (and those aspiring to it) strive to outdo each other in wealth and the conspicuous display of wealth. This emulation drives a continuous cycle of accumulation and consumption as each individual seeks to demonstrate their pecuniary strength, social status, and power.
4. *Repugnance to futility and purposeful leisure*: Despite their avoidance of productive labor, members of the leisure class have a repugnance to activities they perceive as futile. Though unproductive economically, their leisure activities are purposefully chosen to display status, cultivate personal and social connections, and demonstrate mastery or excellence in socially valued fields. These activities, ranging from sports to intellectual pursuits, are chosen for their ability to signify leisure and wealth.
5. *Social stratification and exclusivity*: The behaviors and consumption patterns of the leisure class serve to create and reinforce *social stratification*. The leisure class maintains its exclusivity and dominance by setting standards of decorum, taste, and leisure activity that are exclusive and difficult for lower classes to mimic or afford. This stratification is not static; it evolves as the leisure class adopts new forms of consumption and leisure to distinguish itself from those classes that might be gaining economic ground.
6. *Elaborate standards of decency and decorum*: The leisure class adheres to an elaborate set of standards concerning proper behavior, etiquette, dress, and speech, indicating class membership. These standards are not merely personal preferences but social signals reinforcing the class's exclusivity and status. The complexity of these standards means that only those raised within the leisure class — or those who have invested considerable effort in assimilating these norms — can navigate them successfully, thereby reinforcing class boundaries.

In summary, the leisure class is defined by its strategic engagement in and abstention from certain activities and behaviors to maintain and display its social status. The leisure class establishes and reinforces its dominance and prestige within the social hierarchy through the mechanisms of exemption from productive labor, vicarious leisure, conspicuous consumption, pecuniary emulation, and adherence to elaborate social codes. These characteristics are interdependent, each reinforcing the other in a comprehensive social and economic signaling system that sustains the leisure class's position at the apex of society.

Thorstein Veblen's *Theory of the Leisure Class* does not explicitly define the non-leisure class, but it can be characterized based on the contrasts to the leisure class. The non-leisure class primarily consists of individuals and families directly engaged in productive labor, especially manual and industrial labor. This social group is distinguished by *its necessity for work for subsistence* and is characterized by a lower standard of living and more utilitarian consumption than the leisure class. Contrasting with the leisure class, I identify 10 characteristics of the non-leisure class:

1. *Engagement in productive labor*: The non-leisure class is primarily characterized by its direct involvement in productive labor, especially manual and industrial labor. This class is responsible for the actual production of goods and services, contrasting sharply with the leisure class, which is defined by an exemption from such labor. Their engagement in work is a necessity for *subsistence* rather than a choice to maintain social status.
2. *Lower standard of living*: Compared to the leisure class, the non-leisure class experiences a lower standard of living. Their consumption is primarily driven by necessity and the requirements for basic comfort, without the surplus for conspicuous consumption or the accumulation of wealth and property that defines the leisure class.
3. *Motivated by subsistence needs*: The primary motivation for the non-leisure class is securing the means of subsistence. Unlike the leisure class, driven by pecuniary emulation and the desire for social prestige through wealth accumulation, the non-leisure class focuses on meeting basic needs and maintaining a livelihood.
4. *Less influenced by pecuniary emulation*: While still subject to the societal pressures of pecuniary emulation to some extent, the non-leisure class is less directly influenced by this competitive pursuit of wealth for status. Their limited means restrict their ability to engage in conspicuous consumption, leading them to find value and self-esteem in aspects of life other than monetary wealth.
5. *Different consumption patterns*: The non-leisure class allocates a larger proportion of their income to necessities, with much less left for

discretionary spending on status goods. Their consumption choices are more utilitarian, emphasizing utility and necessity over the status signaling of leisure class consumption.

6. *Lack of exemption from labor*: The *defining* feature of the leisure class — exemption from labor — is precisely what the non-leisure class lacks. Their daily lives are significantly occupied by labor, both a source of subsistence and a marker of their lower status compared to the leisurely lifestyles of the upper class.
7. *Limited social mobility*: Opportunities for upward social mobility are constrained for the non-leisure class. The accumulation of wealth and property, crucial for gaining status and esteem in Veblen's analysis, remains a significant challenge due to their engagement in less valued forms of labor and limited economic resources.
8. *Communal orientation and self-worth*: In contrast to the leisure class's individualistic and competitive ethos, non-leisure class members may exhibit a more communal orientation, valuing cooperation and collective effort. Their sense of self-worth might derive less from pecuniary achievement and more from contributions to the community, workmanship, and ethical or religious values.
9. *Aspiration and influence*: Despite the differences in lifestyle and opportunities, members of the non-leisure class may still aspire to the status and consumption patterns of the leisure class. This aspiration, influenced by societal norms and the visibility of leisure class lifestyles, can impact the values and behaviors of the non-leisure class, even if full emulation remains out of reach.
10. *Role in the industrial system*: The non-leisure class forms the backbone of the industrial system through their labor. They are essential to the functioning of the economy, creating goods and services that sustain societal operations and the leisure class's lifestyle.

In sum, the non-leisure class, as implied by Veblen's critique of the leisure class, is defined by their *necessary* engagement in productive labor, a *lower* standard of living, motivations driven by basic needs, and a *separate set* of values and aspirations shaped by their economic circumstances and social position. Their characteristics contrast with the leisure class, highlighting the divisions and dynamics of social stratification in Veblen's analysis.

We summarize the aforementioned discussion in Table 1.

Table 1. Veblen's leisure class and the non-leisure class compared.

Characteristics	Leisure Class	Non-Leisure
Pursuit of social status	Both classes seek social status and prestige	
Role in social structure	Each class plays a critical role within the social and economic structures	
Engagement in labor	Exempt from productive labor	Directly involved in productive labor, especially manual and industrial work
Standard of living	High; affords conspicuous consumption and wealth accumulation	Lower; primarily focused on subsistence and basic comfort
Motivation	Driven by pecuniary emulation and the desire for prestige through wealth	Motivated by basic needs and subsistence, with less influence from pecuniary emulation
Consumption patterns	Engages in conspicuous consumption beyond necessities for comfort or survival	Consumes based on utility and necessity, with a larger portion of income spent on essentials
Social mobility	High social standing and status are often reinforced through inheritance and exclusive networks	Limited opportunities for upward social mobility due to economic constraints and access to education
Social norms and etiquette	Follows elaborate standards indicating class membership; values exclusivity	Adheres to more practical norms, not bound by the leisure class's codes; values accessibility
Position in status and power	Occupies the top of the social hierarchy, maintaining status through wealth and leisure activities	Positioned lower in the hierarchy, their labor sustains the leisure class's lifestyle and consumption
Values and self-worth	Esteem derived from wealth, leisure, and exclusivity	May find self-worth in community contribution, workmanship, and ethical values beyond wealth

Followers of Veblen

Veblen's work is now more than a century old. Before I reflect on the applicability of his ideas to the current economic and societal context, I will passingly note that his ideas have influenced numerous streams of scholarly thought in the US, particularly in the 20th century. For the purpose of the argument developed in this book, I will be *selective* and comment on his intellectual influence only on *four* streams of scholarship: (1) institutional economics, (2) sociology, (3) culture, and (4) technology studies.

Institutional economics

Veblen could be viewed as a member of the then-emerging field of "old" institutional economists in the US, which included luminaries like Rexford Tugwell, John M. Clark, and Wesley Mitchell.[7] These economists directed the attention of economists to the social embeddedness of transactions. For example, institutional economists pointed out that the market (a crucial concept in all of economics), which involves social norms, and customs, which exchange relations, and which consciously organized information networks, itself requires theoretical explanation (Dosi, 1988; Hodgson, 1988). Similarly, according to them, the institution of private property itself requires explanation; without addressing the emergence of these rights and their (sociological) roots, they cannot be satisfactorily understood.

At the risk of simplification, I enumerate three of Veblen's contributions to economics. First, as I noted earlier, he was a pioneer of the field of institutional economics. Second, he provided a set of *new concepts*, lenses through which we can view the economic landscape. The most prominent among these concepts are (1) "conspicuous consumption" or the practice of buying and using goods or services to display one's social status or wealth, and (2) "Veblen goods," which are products that consumers consider status symbols and whose demand increases as their

[7] Institutional economists in the US, which included luminaries like Rexford Tugwell, John M. Clark, and Wesley Mitchell, active in the early 20th century, challenged neoclassical assumptions by emphasizing real-world institutions, historical context, and empirical methods. Tugwell influenced New Deal policies, Clark developed the theory of workable competition, and Mitchell was a pioneer of business cycle research.

price increases. Third, he highlighted the role of income inequality in society, which sometimes prevents people from participating in the economy. Although Veblen's ideas were claimed to have inspired Franklin Roosevelt's New Deal,[8] they went into oblivion for several decades. The sixties witnessed a renewed interest in his thought, notably with the founding of the Association for Evolutionary Economics[9] (Dostaler, 2003).

Sociologists

In retrospect, we can see that just as much as he was an economist, Veblen was also a sociologist. He commented on the US social scene, leading C. Wright Mills[10] to hail him as one of the foremost social thinkers of his time (Mestrovic, 2016). Sociology, however, discovered Veblen late, leading Bergen to comment that academic sociologists began to take note of his contributions to their field only shortly before his death (Bergen, 1973). His *Leisure Class* provided a theory of social stratification, one of the central ideas in sociology. He advanced the concept of *pecuniary emulation*, a term that captured the economic efforts of an individual from a lower economic class to surpass a rich person's socio-economic status. Veblen went further, arguing that the pecuniary struggle to acquire and exhibit wealth, thereby gaining status, is the driving force behind the development of culture and society. In this sense, he offered a vision of strategic change different from Karl Marx, although the latter may have had many more adherents in sociology.

---

[8]The New Deal was a series of federal programs launched by President Franklin D. Roosevelt in response to the Great Depression. It transformed the role of government in economic life, introducing social security, labor protections, and banking reforms.

[9]Association for Evolutionary Economics (AFEE) is an academic organization dedicated to the study and promotion of institutional and evolutionary economics, building on the legacy of economists like Veblen and Commons. It was founded in 1965 and publishes the *Journal of Economic Issues*.

[10]C. Wright Mills is a sociologist best known for *The Power Elite* (1956). Mills examined how a small group of military, corporate, and political leaders dominated American decision-making. He also developed the concept of the "sociological imagination."

Cultural commentators

Because Veblen exposed the behavior patterns of the leisure class, specifically their lifestyles, he has sometimes been called an anthropologist (Reisman, 2018) or cultural sociologist (Mestrovic, 2019). His ideas, however, are often co-opted by students of contemporary cultures, the field itself sometimes called cultural studies. In particular, I would like to mention three. First, and not surprisingly, because Veblen directed attention to the consumption patterns of different classes of individuals in society, there have been efforts to uncover the dress, external behaviors (e.g., eating habits), and other consumption patterns of different classes of people. Second, and perhaps more importantly, his work inspired many women's studies scholars. In the following, I quote Martha Benta[11] at some length to give a flavor of Veblen's influence:

> One of the more startling aspects of Veblen's assessment is the stress he places on the male's 'ownership' of women achieved through the retention of entrenched customs. In Veblen's overview, the story of the Rape of the Sabine Women cannot be stuffed away in the musty archives of ancient history. No matter what refinements have been added to contemporary modes of seizure, men continue to appropriate women to affirm their sex's prerogatives. Veblen called upon recent disclosures by anthropologists that the women in the most primitive societies once wielded great power. It was the later 'advanced' societies controlled by members of the warrior class that set the pattern for centuries to come. As for the wives of late nineteenth-century business tycoons, they were flaunted as trophies, their bared bosoms draped with jewels, as proof of their men's wealth and success. (p. xviii)

And finally, and perhaps more recently, Veblen has inspired environmental sociologists, who began to pay attention to his knowledge and interest in natural resources.

---

[11]Martha Banta is Professor Emerita of English at UCLA and a prominent scholar of American literature and culture. Her work explores themes such as gender, aesthetics, and modernity in the 19th and early 20th centuries. Notable publications include *Imaging American Women* and *Taylored Lives*, both of which analyze the intersection of literature, visual culture, and social ideals in US history.

Technology studies

Veblen saw technology as a major force in societal change (see Philip Klein,1999). He was concerned with the wastefulness he observed in institutions and regarded technology as a means to ameliorate some of the waste. He codified that idea in his intriguing concept, *Veblenian dichotomy*. The dichotomy puts forth two functions — ceremonial and instrumental, both of which are performed by institutions. As Veblen saw it, some institutions use technology for "ceremonial" purposes — in other words, wastefully. Veblen believed that institutions should use technology in a more instrumental way, one that is purposeful.

Veblen's analysis reflected his own context of industrial capitalism and was built on the assumption that new technologies introduced by engineers would fundamentally alter social relations and institutions. Veblen maintained that because institutions determine their use, technologies can be employed to reduce institutional waste. Because of these views, he has sometimes been characterized as a technological determinist (Brette, 2003). While not explicitly using the phrase "technological determinism" in his work, Veblen's writings laid the foundation for this concept by emphasizing the role of technological advancements in shaping social structures and economic systems.

Critics of Veblen

It is not surprising that, given the broad sweep of Veblen's ideas, he has incited wide-ranging intellectual criticism. I will mention three of these, foreshadowing their reference in later chapters in this book:

Marxist critique: Prominent Marxist economists like Paul Sweezy, Paul Baran, and E.K. Hunt[12] have criticized Veblen for his focus on "conspicuous consumption" and "pecuniary emulation," thus underplaying the central role of class struggle in driving economic change, which, of course, is a cornerstone of Marxist theory. The list of specific critics is long, and the range of criticisms developed by several Marxist economists, ranging from the lack of a clear explanation of economic crises, inadequate theory of capital accumulation, business cycle, etc., and even racism.

[12]Prominent Marxist economists like Paul Sweezy, Paul Baran, and E.K. Hunt: These economists developed critical perspectives on capitalism rooted in Marxist theory. Sweezy co-founded *Monthly Review*, Baran co-authored *Monopoly Capital*, and Hunt was known for synthesizing Marxist and institutionalist traditions.

Technological determinism: Some social scientists have been uncomfortable with Veblen's upholding of technology as a factor in social change. They argue that unlike actor network theory (as an example) it neglects the influence of social, cultural, and political factors that actively shape how technology is developed and adopted. These critics maintain that human agency shapes technological change, and they disavow the notion that technology created social outcomes.

Fuzzy concepts: Arguably, one of the challenges that scholars experience is the difficulty in distinguishing between leisure and work. It is context-dependent and changes with the times, and sometimes depends on the motivation of the individuals. In other words, finding proxies for the distinction for empirical work, which sometimes privileges quantitative analysis, is arduous, and this has limited hypothesis testing of Veblen's ideas.

The Current Context

At the beginning of this chapter, I mentioned that Veblen developed his thesis about the leisure class in the Gilded Age — late in the 19th century, in the early stages of the industrial era. Compared to that age, the societal landscape in the US today looks vastly different. In Table 2, I have documented some simple statistics about the US to drive home the point.

A glance at the table will tell us:

1. The US has grown significantly over the years, and so has the GDP. Indeed, the nominal per capita GDP has shown a significant increase over the years.
2. From a predominantly agricultural economy, the US has become a service economy, both in terms of where individuals are employed as well as in terms of contribution to the GDP.
3. While in 1890 the US was emerging as a science and technology leader, by 2020, the US is the preeminent leader in these fields.

Of course, it is impossible to document all the changes, but it would be easy to see that the contemporary US economy looks vastly different from that of the late 18th century. I am sure these statistics, and the resultant conclusions, will surprise no one, and I could have picked up a lot of

Table 2. Selected macroeconomic differences between Veblen's time and now.

Factor / Year	**1890**	**2020**
Population	63 M	331 M
GDP	15.6 billion	20.93 trillion
Major economic sectors	Agriculture Manufacturing and Mining	The service sector (76.4%), Industry (17.61%), and Agriculture 0.94%
Average wage	13.70 cents	28.16 dollars
Employment in: agriculture industrial sector	Highest in agriculture industry next	Highest in the service sector, then in manufacturing
Science & technology leadership	Emerging as a global leader	The preeminent global leader

others, but I want to drive home the point that what we call work — or the activities associated with work — have significantly changed from the time of Veblen.

Against this backdrop, Veblen's writing may seem quaint to many readers. But this difference sets up one of the primary motivations of this book.

Of the many changes over more than a century, I will spotlight three major ones pertinent to this book: (1) Shifts in technology, (2) the ways in which work itself has changed, and (3) changes in the way we think of leisure.

Shifts in technology

At the time of Veblen's writing, the world was undergoing a tectonic shift from the agrarian era to industrial civilization, triggered by the Industrial Revolution in Europe. Although the US was a latecomer to this shift, many of the societal shifts were experienced here. Just like in the UK,[13] these societal shifts were often captured in the literature in the first half of

[13] In the UK, authors like Charles Dickens had already vividly portrayed the horrors of industrialization. Although not as influential as these authors, Sinclair pioneered the style of muckraking in the US.

the 20th century. As one example, Upton Sinclair's *The Jungle*[14] vividly portrayed the migration of people from rural to urban areas, the rise of the nuclear family, and the inhuman consequences of automation in the meat-packing industry. Veblen's writings gave voice to the emerging differentiation of society into the leisure and working classes, with the leisure class looking down upon the working class, especially those in industrial workplaces.

The world has moved on: In the US at least, the last century witnessed the New Deal (which Veblen had reportedly influenced), the design of worker protections (e.g., OSHA), and a technological change of a kind that moved us from an industrial to an information society, none of which could have been anticipated in the late 19th century. All these developments have had far-reaching changes in our conception of work and leisure.

Work

Significant shifts have occurred in work and work practices in the US over the years. First, new job categories have emerged. A recent National Bureau of Economic Research paper demonstrated that "the majority of current employment is in new job specialties introduced after 1940, but the locus of new work creation has shifted — from middle-paid production and clerical occupations over 1940–1980, to high-paid professional and, secondarily, low-paid services since 1980" (Autor *et al.*, 2022). The authors go on to demonstrate that technological innovation has been a major factor in the creation of these jobs. Second, work hours in the United States have decreased significantly from 1900 to 2020. In 1900, the average work week was 60 hours per week, but by 1920, it had gone down to 48 (with 6 working days a week). By 1940, partly stimulated by the passage of the Fair Labor Standards Act (1938), which limited the workweek to 44 hours, and later the 40-hour workweek, which was also

[14]Upton Sinclair's *The Jungle* was published in 1906. *The Jungle* exposed unsanitary conditions in the US.. meatpacking industry and led to public outcry and food safety reforms. Although Sinclair intended to highlight labor exploitation, its impact was strongest on consumer protection legislation.

passed into law (1940). In addition to shorter workdays, workers have also gained more holidays, vacations, sick days, and personal leave. Third, industrial corporations have attempted to infuse work with greater flexibility with programs such as flextime during the 1970s, and more recently after the coronavirus pandemic, by allowing workers to work from home.

Leisure

Earlier, I had referred to one of the criticisms leveled against Veblen — the fuzziness of the concept of leisure. To be fair to Veblen, he was referring to the leisure *class*, not specifically leisure. The scholarly criticism, the fuzziness of the concept — centered on issues centering upon the accurate "measurement" of leisure. Without discounting its importance, I would like to add that even the "popular" conceptions of leisure and leisure class have undergone significant shifts over the century. Let me set forth three illustrations:

1. Because the US economy has expanded over the century, the number of "rich" people has also grown. One data point suggests that whereas in 1990 there were fewer than 70 billionaires, there were over 700 billionaires by 2023.[15] In fact, the term "trust fund babies" has emerged in recent years to connote individuals born into money without working for it — a term often used pejoratively. However, some evidence also suggests that not all of the rich in 2023 are born into money. Also, other data suggest that many of the very rich are indeed among the most hardworking, blurring the distinction between the leisure and the working class.
2. New categories of people have been ascribed the dubious distinction of belonging to the leisure class. For example, professors in higher education in the US have increasingly been seen as part of an "academic leisure class," leading one academic to offer a lengthy rebuttal:

[15] Vedder, R. (2018). The Academic Leisure Class: The Underutilization of College Resources, *Forbes*, December 6, 2018.

Nearly 120 years ago the eccentric sociologist/economist Thorstein Veblen wrote his *Theory of the Leisure Class*. A strong case can be made that today, higher education is an academic leisure class — many students and professors working embarrassingly few hours a year. It is often argued America's universities are inefficient, suggesting employees produce relatively little of value for each hour worked. There is some truth to that assertion, but there is the second problem: students and many employees don't work very many hours. To be sure, there are many exceptions, and I know professors and some students who work long days, sometimes on weekends, researching, teaching, writing, and advising.[16]

3. Our views of what constitutes leisure have developed over the years, leading us to a more nuanced view than a simplistic one that equates leisure with non-work. I will cite two instances of this development. First, scholars began to distinguish active from "passive" forms of leisure. Evidence is marshaled to show that the wealthy spend their time in remarkably similar ways to the general population, but they engage in more active leisure. Active leisure included praying, socializing, intimate relations, exercise, hobbies, and volunteering, whereas passive leisure included watching TV, napping and resting, relaxing, and doing nothing (Smeets *et al.* 2020). Second, some groups of scholars have tried to distinguish between forms of leisure: Social (e.g., socializing with friends and family), cognitive (e.g., engaging in mentally stimulating activities), and physical leisure (e.g., physical activities including yoga).[17]

On the whole, these and related developments should lead us to rethink the developing conceptions of leisure, and by extension, "work." In the next section, I would like to outline *one* perspective of what distinguishes work from leisure, and in the later chapters, develop the theme of the possibility of a workless society.

---

[16] Alicia Sparks Akers (2020). The 3 Types of Active Leisure, *PsychCentral.*

[17] Vedder, R. (2018) The Academic Leisure Class: The Underutilization of College Resources, *Forbes*, December 6, 2018. Smeets, P., Whillans, A., Bekkers, R., and Norton, M. I. (2020). Time use and happiness of millionaires: Evidence from the Netherlands. *Social Psychological and Personality Science*, *11*(3), 295–307.

Leisure as a Metaphor

Just how does one distinguish work from leisure? In common parlance, the term 'work' has had both positive and negative connotations. In the positive sense, work has been considered to be one of the means by which men and women shape their environments, transform, and cultivate them to obtain what they need and desire. In the negative sense, work is thought of as a constraint — alienation exerted by a dominating power upon those who have to work. In his classic work, Veblen employed the term, leisure class, to offer a differentiation of society into leisure and working classes. Recall that the working class he referred to was employed primarily in industrial settings.

At its very core, industrial work is a contract between an 'employee' and an 'employer', where the employee receives a wage in exchange for work. For Veblen, the concept of work was confined to industrial settings and was central to the distinction between leisure and the working class. As we have seen, the leisure class is exempt from productivity, especially manual labor. Not only does the leisure class avoid productive labor, but its members also find repugnant these activities they perceive as futile. Though unproductive economically, their activities are purposefully chosen to display status, reinforcing the status differentiation in society.

Although Veblen's characterization of the leisure class includes consumption-related and sociocultural elements, he allows us to identify three critical characteristics of work that distinguish it from leisure: (1) necessity, (2) transactional, and (3) constraints.

Necessity: An individual enters into an employment contract primarily out of necessity, i.e., to satisfy his/her and their family's *material* needs. Although they may have several options, the degree of satisfaction of their material needs is a driver of their very consideration of those options. Stated differently, without employment, individuals may find it difficult to meet their lower-level needs.[18] Necessity sets it apart from a leisure activity, which an individual may undertake purely out of intrinsic or other reasons.

Transactional: By its very nature, an employment contract involves an agreement between two individuals and is thus transactional. Because

---

[18] Lower-level need in the sense of Abraham Maslow.

the agreement is negotiated, the relative power of the parties is offered as an explanation for the outcomes. Indeed, a significant aspect of the Marxist critique of capitalist economies in general, and of Veblen in particular, hinges on the ability of capital, given its higher power, to exploit labor.

Constraints: In most cases, the "work" in an industrial setting is subject to several constraints. The most obvious one is the set of constraints imposed by technology. For example, in assembly line jobs, the pace of work is dictated by the movement of the line. Perhaps equally important are the other policies under which an employee works, like the work hours (sometimes starting and ending times each day), drug testing, or restrictions on conflict resolution (around pay or behavior). The employee may not have much control over these rules, but they come as a part of the employment contract.

Table 3 summarizes the three characteristics and how work and leisure differ in terms of these characteristics.

The three factors — necessity, transactional nature, and constraints — enable us to distinguish work from leisure or more accurately non-work. Veblen would most likely agree that individuals undertake leisure activities, not out of necessity to meet some physical needs, but due either to intrinsic needs or social pressures. 'Luxury' activities such as conspicuous consumption may exhibit transactional character, and leaving aside the constraints imposed by technology may involve *willingly* accepted constraints. Thus, the central facet of the distinction is *necessity*: We undertake work out of necessity, and in doing so, we trade our autonomy for some extrinsic rewards.

Table 3. A comparison between leisure and work.

Characteristics	Work	Leisure
1. Necessity	Yes	No; except for inner compulsion
2. Transactional	Always	Not necessary
3. Constraints	Imposed by organizations	Voluntarily agreed upon

In developing this book's thesis, I diverge from Veblen in three fundamental ways.

1. Although I owe a significant intellectual debt to Veblen — and this chapter is a testimonial to that — I use leisure as "metaphor," using the term to connote *non-work*. As I indicated before, the developing conception of leisure after Veblen has become immensely complex, and leisure now includes diverse activities, certainly almost all forms of non-work.
2. Unlike Veblen, I focus solely on work and how technological developments underway may enable us to *emancipate* ourselves from the coercive necessity of work. I am less focused on conspicuous consumption, or the bases of social stratification that were outlined by Veblen.
3. Third, Veblen's writings are anchored in the empirical details of his social context, the Gilded Age, and in this sense, he was captive of the evidence in front of him. His concepts, brilliant though they be, were forged to capture the ambience of his time and thus closer to observable reality. Being anchored in the current context, I have attempted to tease out one of the major assumptions driving the decisions about our own society.

In this sense, in this book, I am departing from the extant scholarship in two ways. First, I peer under the veil of concepts to capture a key assumption, in this case about work, to emancipate our focus from the *coercive* influence of evidence. Second, and related to the above, I undertake an exercise in assumption analysis, maintaining that understanding key assumptions offers one approach to *imagining* societal possibilities.

In the next chapter, I will outline how, in the US, the concept of work changed both because of large-scale societal changes and our scholarly writings.

References

Bergen, T. J. (1973). The sociological mind of Thorstein Veblen. *Journal of Thought*, 224–233.

Brette, O. (2003). Thorstein Veblen's theory of institutional change: Beyond technological determinism. *European Journal of the History of Economic Thought*, 10(3), 455–477.

Dosi, G. (1988). Institutions and markets in a dynamic world. *The Manchester School*, 56(2), 119–146.

Hodgson, G. M. (1988). Economics and institutions: a manifesto for modern institutional economics. In *Economics and Institutions*. Philadelphia: University of Pennsylvania Press.

Klein, P. A. (1999). The theory of the leisure class, inspiration for the new millennium. *History of Economic Ideas*, 85–98.

Mestrovic, S. G. (2019). Thorstein Veblen and cultural sociology. In *Handbuch Kultursoziologie: Band 1: Begriffe–Kontexte–Perspektiven–Autor_innen* (pp. 691–696). Wiesbaden: Springer Fachmedien Wiesbaden.

Smeets, P., Whillans, A., Bekkers, R., and Norton, M. I. (2020). Time use and happiness of millionaires: Evidence from the Netherlands. *Social Psychological and Personality Science*, 11(3), 295–307.

Chapter 3

Perspectives on Work

Abstract

In the preceding chapter, I noted that the concept of leisure that lay at the center of Veblen's theory of the leisure class has later been elaborated by many others. In this chapter, I summarize how our conception of work has also changed over the years. Historians have described the evolution of work over centuries into the beginning of the 20th century. They have suggested that changes in work are a reflection of major transitions in society. In the 20th century, management scholars mooted the idea that work can be designed to promote organizational efficiency. Later in the 20th century, modern-day futurists highlighted the central role played by technology in the design of work. We build on this connection in the next chapters to argue for the possibility of a workless society.

What is Work?

Because most people spend a significant part of their waking life working, the story of work is to a great extent the history of humankind.[1] The term "work" is thus so commonplace that on the face of it, the question "What is work?" may have a ring of absurdity to it. However, over the years, the

[1] Lucassen, J. (2021). *The Story of Work*, Yale University Press. I have borrowed the history of work prior to the 20th century from this magisterial work.

term has been a topic of contestation, with different meanings attributed to it, just like the concept of leisure covered in the last chapter. These contestations can be classified based on two of their prominent attributes: breadth and perspective.

Breadth: Some, such as Tilly,[2] have regarded work in a very broad sense, considering any human effort that adds *use value* to goods and services as work. They argue that most work takes place outside of regular jobs, and that this was the state of affairs before the 20th century. Their definition thus embraces housework, and they only exclude "purely destructive (e.g., soldiering), expressive (e.g., singing) or consumptive (e.g., eating) acts" from being labeled work. Unlike these universalists, others have been selective, focusing primarily on wage work. Of course, some of these others have dealt with slave labor or self-employment instead of wage labor.

Perspective: A second distinction is the perspective that undergirds the definition of work. The most common is the viewpoint of the market economy, primarily in economics. The economists focus on market transactions. Here, work is primarily confined to wage labor, and the market mediates the wages received by the worker in return for work performed for the employer. Unlike economists, sociologists such as Tilly opt for use-value, which enables them to consider forms of work that are not considered work from a market perspective: e.g., housework of various kinds, or women's work. Market perspective leads its protagonists to address issues related to wage determination. Instead, sociologists focus on social relations, which enable them to address a broader set of activities at work.

In addition to market transactions, sociologists have identified two relations that are central to understanding work: vertical and horizontal relations. Vertical relations refer to "opposition" in market societies,

[2]Charles Tilly (May 27, 1929–April 29, 2008) was an American sociologist, political scientist, and historian who wrote on the relationship between politics and society. He has been described as "the founding father of 21st-century sociology" and "one of the world's preeminent sociologists and historians." He published widely across topics, such as urban sociology, state formation, democracy, social movements, labor, and inequality. He was an influential proponent of large-scale historical social science research. Tarrow wrote about his contribution in an essay "The Contributions of Charles Tilly to the Social Sciences," in *Contemporary Sociology* in 2018.

between employer and employee, slave owner and slave, and citizen and state. Labor historians typically focus on this dimension, highlighting employment contracts, as well as work incentives, "the ways in which an employer can encourage his worker to perform better" (Lucassen, 2021, p. 7). Horizontal relations refer to the cooperative actions between workers: people work together with others, and their mutual relationships are an intrinsic part of work relationships. Of course, power relationships are much greater in vertical relationships than in horizontal relations.

Before I review these conceptions against the distinction between work and leisure referred to in the previous chapter, I want to acknowledge that much of the scholarship has underscored the shifting nature of work across the millennia. *Work as we know it today was not the work humans did centuries ago*, a point that can be illustrated by a broad sweep of the history of work.

Perspective I: Historical Evolution of Work: Lucassen's Model

In 2021, Jan Lucassen, a Dutch historian who specializes in the history of labor, published a masterpiece, *The Story of Work: A New History of Humankind*, a global history of work, from prehistoric times until the present. I use this much-acclaimed book to illustrate the vast transformation that has taken place in our work patterns and also our understanding of work.

Lucassen's six-period model spans the time period from the emergence of *homo sapiens* (700,000 years ago) to the period that started with the *Industrial Revolution* (2000 CE). I will take the reader through a whirlwind tour of the very long timeframe he covered, spending more time on the first four. I will summarize his first four periods in Table 1.

First period: By far the longest, this period begins from the emergence of *home sapiens*, nearly 700,000 years ago, to the Neolithic Revolution. During this period, there was no distinction between human and animal attempts to survive. The individual lived within a household, households formed bands, and all work took place within these units. The primary activity was the daily procurement of food by hunting (including fishing) and gathering of food, childcare and alloparenting, fire management, shelter construction, and clothing production. This activity was enabled by the development of standardized stone tools, and hence, over time,

Table 1. Summary of Lucassen's model: The first four periods.

	First period	Second period	Third period	Fourth period
Time	70,000 years ago	Agrarian revolution 12,000 years ago	7,000 years ago	500 BCE
Tools used	Primarily implements	Included plows and agrarian-related equipment	New technologies in metallurgy, construction methods, agriculture,	Coins and Monetary transactions, written documents, and construction plans Continuation of previous era trends
Division of labor	Between males and females	Deepening division	Urban and rural distinctions	Heterogenization of work locations
Social units	Household	Families	The role of polities	The emergence of institutions: guilds and craft organizations
Work activities	Procurement of food, childcare, alloparenting, shelter, and safety	Farming and animal husbandry	Metalworking, construction, and administrative work	New forms of work from market transactions, such as trade and commerce

tool-making became an important activity. Tools included hand axes and cleavers, spear throwers, nests for hunting and fishing, eyed needles, strings for weaving, pottery, canoes and boats, grindstones and millstones, and wire spears. Life and work exhibited mobile patterns across various environments, typically ranging from 300 sq. km; there was seasonal movement as well. There was a division of labor between males and females, and cooperation was emphasized, but because there was limited specialization, the division of labor was flexible. There were reciprocal sharing systems and marriage-based alliances between bands.

Second period: The Neolithic or agrarian revolution, 12,000 years ago, offered opportunities for obtaining and hoarding food. Alongside cooperation, subordination was being created, but Lucassen disavows a causal link between the agricultural revolution and social inequality. Work activities broadened from hunting and gathering to include arable farming (plowing, sowing, weeding, irrigating, harvesting), and animal husbandry (herding, feeding, watering, pasturing, milking, breeding, and slaughtering). Pottery making and weaving emerged as specialized crafts in some regions. The tools included plows pulled by animals, sickles and scythes for harvesting crops, baskets, shovels and tools for irrigation, pottery wheels and kilns for creating ceramic vessels, spindles and looms for weaving wool and plant fibers. There was increased division of labor between men and women, and some regional exchange of goods between farming and hunter-gatherer communities. Work shifted from mobile hunter-gathering bands to sedentary agricultural villages, and work was centered around permanent dwellings, fields, and pastures. New technologies were developed for: domestication of plants (grains, legumes, fruit trees), irrigation (canals, reservoirs, water lifting devices), and textile production (spinning and weaving technologies).

Third period: With the emergence of cities some 7,000 years ago, the division of labor between urban and rural areas became possible. Alongside individuals and households, polities with their institutions became indispensable, which redistributed surplus production. Thus, work activities enlarged from agriculture (farming and herding), metal working (copper, bronze iron), and construction (pyramids and temples), to include administrative work (scribes), military service, religious work, and domestic labor. Some forms of maritime work, artisanal craft, and mining also came into existence. Institutions played a role in the design of work, with state-directed, temple-based and military hierarchies influencing the work activity. New tools came into practice: metal-working and construction tools, navigation equipment, and mining tools; administrative tools (e.g., clay tokens, seals); pottery making and textile tools. Lucassen noted that work organization was beginning to be influenced by the state, temples, and even the military. Slave labor, early market systems, and craft specialization also began to emerge during this period. Work was now conducted in a multiplicity of locations: agricultural fields, urban centers, temple complexes, construction sites, military facilities, mining areas, maritime ports, rural settlements, and, of course, household spaces. Significant technology developments took place in metallurgy, construction methods, irrigation systems, agriculture, maritime, mining, and building technologies, and early writing systems.

Fourth period: Starting around 500 BCE, a renewal in human transactions took place with the invention of small coins (What Lucassen calls "deep monetization"). This facilitated market transactions (e.g., payment of wages or purchasing daily food and craft products from the self-employed), thus creating new forms of work. Thus, work activities included public works and trade and commerce, in addition to agricultural labor, artisanal crafts, construction, maritime and military work, mining, religious and domestic service prevalent in the previous era. Newer tools emerged: coinage and monetary instruments, written records and documents, construction plans and templates, while tool innovations were continuing in agricultural, construction, mining, maritime, and textiles. The heterogenization of locations of work continued, and markets and trading centers, and royal state facilities also became scenes of activity. Similarly, new developments continued in many spheres, but most notably in monetary systems and manufacturing sites. Guilds and craft organizations appeared as work became organized. Just like activity itself, the era witnessed the persistence of many forms of organizations in which work was carried out: military hierarchies, religious hierarchies, and state bureaucracies.

Fifth period (1500–1800 CE): In what Lucassen calls the time of globalization, the competition between political entities led to widely differing forms of labor in different parts of the world. Heterogenization of work activities and locations in which they were carried out persisted, and so did innovative activity in tool making.

Sixth period: Starting with the *Industrial Revolution*, the division of work and skills created innumerable new occupations, wholly eradicating others. The Industrial Revolution triggered the transition from a labor-intensive to a capital-intensive form of activity. Mechanization, steam as the new energy source, inventions in chemistry and biotechnology all lay at the core of this transition. Work became associated with factory work. Lucassen pointed out that independent and unfree labor became less important for the market.

The historical models, Lucassen being an exemplar, locate work in the broadest societal context. We could infer that they view the newer tools as solutions humans forge to solve their daily work-related problems. The models typically invoke evolutionary processes to explain change, and from this perspective, changes in work are seen as an evolutionary process in step with the broader changes in society.

Perspective II: Engineering the Work for Organizational Outcomes

As the primary venue for the origin of work-related practices shifted from Europe to the US in the 20th century, a radically new set of ideas about work began to be advanced by various American scholar-practitioners. These ideas are still in vogue, precluding the possibility of arranging them in stages as done by Lucassen in his historical model.

These ideas also spurred the origin of the emerging academic discipline of management. At the center of these ideas, and also of the management discipline, is the assertion that managers can *deliberately* bring about changes in work practices and context to enhance organizational effectiveness. Not only are work activities not subject merely to evolutionary processes in society but managers can also actually control them with their own decisions. There have been, of course, debates about the right criterion of effectiveness, but without wading into those debates in this book, I will identify five major schools of thought that share the assumption.[3]

Scientific management: Frederick Winslow Taylor is often credited with the idea that work can be *scientifically studied* and altered for higher productivity. He promoted his ideas in the early part of the 20th century when the Industrial Revolution and the mass production it triggered were sweeping the United States. Quite soon, others such as Frank and Lillian Gilbreth and Henry Gantt also became leading scholar-practitioners of the school. Whereas Taylor developed the core principles of scientific management, focusing on optimizing work processes and standardized

---

[3]The central debates among three of the schools are covered in my earlier book, *Organization Theory: A Strategic Approach*, co-authored with Ragu Nath.

methods, Frank and Lillian Gilbreth[4] developed motion studies, analyzing worker movements to identify inefficiencies and improve productivity. Henry Gantt is credited with developing the Gantt chart,[5] a visual tool for project planning and tracking.

Scientific management (SM) scholars promoted process efficiency as the key criterion of organizational effectiveness, to the exclusion of market and human variables. As these approaches became popular, modern-day industrial engineering departments in many US engineering schools grew out of an intent to disseminate scientific management tools to students. As the SM approaches were implemented in organizations, their use also incited fear of job loss among the employees. This led to a reaction and saw the emergence of the human relations school.

Human relations (HR) school: Mostly developed in the US, HR schools not only arose partly as an ideological counterfoil to SM but also as a reaction to the excesses of the implementation of SM approaches in organizations. Public intellectuals like Mary Parker Follett[6] and scholar philosophers like Elton Mayo[7] — folks who played central roles in the emergence of HR school — had always advocated for an enlightened workplace that met not only the production demands of organizations but also served as humane places. And in the 1930s, when migration to the cities triggered by the industrial revolution was in full swing, and individual employees spent a major part of their life in the workplace, the need to humanize the workplace was of great interest to these intellectuals. Perhaps more consequential was the rapid adoption of production

---

[4]Pioneers of motion study and time efficiency in industrial management, the Gilbreths contributed foundational work to ergonomics and human factors engineering. Lillian Gilbreth was also one of the first female engineers with a Ph.D.

[5]Developed by Henry L. Gantt in the early 1900s, the Gantt chart is a project management tool that visually tracks tasks across time. It remains widely used in industrial engineering, software development, and project planning.

[6]Follett was a management theorist and social philosopher who emphasized participatory democracy, group dynamics, and human relations in organizational settings. Her ideas anticipated modern theories of leadership and collaboration.

[7]An Australian psychologist and sociologist best known for the Hawthorne Studies, Mayo helped establish the Human Relations Movement in management. His work showed the psychological and social dimensions of work environments. Fritz J. Roethlisberger collaborated with Elton Mayo on the Hawthorne Studies and co-authored key texts in organizational behavior. He emphasized informal organization and worker satisfaction in improving productivity.

efficiency as *the* major goal of corporations, and the widespread adoption of SM approaches to accomplish that. The anxieties that this created in the workplace were so immense that there was even a Congressional inquiry into the SM practices in organizations.

HR movement got scholarly respectability from the now-famous Hawthorne experiments. Initially started as an SM experiment, the experiments began to produce unanticipated results that led the company to seek help from social scientists, primarily Elton Mayo and his acolyte Roethlisberger from Harvard University, for explanation. Based on this evidence, HR scholars began to argue that the modern workplace is more than an instrument for production, but that it was a community, and that leadership behavior was a causal factor in both productivity and human satisfaction. To use Lucassen's terms, they included 'vertical relations' as a component of work, in addition to the specific activities that were the focus of SM scholars.

The socio-technical system school (ST): Almost contemporaneous with the HR school in the US, the ST School arose in the UK. The school, also focusing on the social side of enterprise, arose from a set of influential field studies done in the UK in various settings typical of the organizations in the Industrial era — e.g., mining, custom shops, mass production factories, and process engineering organizations. Scholars such as Eric Trist,[8] A.K. Rice, and Joanne Woodward played a central role in developing the ideas of ST.

One of the earliest works done in the mining industry alerted scholars to the idea that effective work groups generated significant relations among the members, and these relations were related to their well-being and satisfaction. Unlike the HR school, the UK scholars took authority to be an enduring facet of an organization. Thus, their macro comparative studies demonstrated that the authority systems differed among production types.

---

[8]A founding figure in socio-technical systems theory, Trist worked with the Tavistock Institute to examine how organizations could balance technical efficiency with human well-being. He influenced participatory management models. A.K. Rice was a British psychoanalyst associated with the Tavistock Institute. He developed methods for studying group dynamics and authority structures in organizational settings. Joan Woodward was a pioneer in organization theory. Her seminal work, *Industrial Organization: Theory and Practice*, was originally published in 1965. In contrast to prevailing beliefs at the time, Woodward's book concludes with what is now known as *contingency theory*, that there is no single perfect way to organize any industrial firm. Instead, the best way is *contingent* on the internal and external context.

According to Joan Woodward, who initiated this approach, organizations can be classified as unit or small batch, large batch or mass production, and continuous process. These exhibit different characteristics across factors like employee relations or management style. She laid the groundwork for what is now known as contingency theory, the principle that there is no single perfect way to organize any industrial firm. Instead, the best way is contingent on the internal and external context.

ST scholars promoted the "new" idea that even within an organization with its authority flows, it is possible to jointly optimize both production demands and human satisfaction. They thus focused on what Lucassen terms "horizontal relations." The ST school moved from field studies to interventions in organizations by building groups that matched the technology of production. Among their first intervention was the one in India in the 1950s at a textile mill, where researchers led by introduced changes to work organization within both automatic and non-automatic loom sheds.

Job design school[9]: The job design approaches were initially put forth by social scientists in the US, partly as a reaction to the mechanistic stance of SM that excluded consideration of human elements. These approaches built upon the HR and ST models that preceded them. However, the job design approach was not monolithic and included job rotation, job enlargement, and job enrichment. Job rotation refers to moving employees between different organizational jobs or tasks; job enlargement is adding a more comprehensive range of employee duties that are at a similar skill level; job enrichment increases the complexity of an employee's job by adding additional responsibilities requiring higher-level skills.

Ultimately, applying sociotechnical systems principles led to the development of autonomous work groups (AWG) (Cummings, 1978), teams that are also referred to as semi-autonomous work groups and self-managing teams. Here, the teams carry out a relatively whole task, members have a range of skills, and the team has autonomy over when and how the work is done. Interdependence is also typically recognized as a defining feature of a team (Kiggundu, 1983). AWGs were most popular in Europe, especially Scandinavian countries with a strong history of industrial democratization, although they also spread to the US and beyond.

The technological element of the sociotechnical systems approach has been less present in the job design literature (Parker *et al.*, 2017). Exceptions

---

[9]A recent exhaustive literature review of the topic is available in Parker, S. K., Morgeson, F. P., and Johns, G. (2017). One hundred years of work design research: Looking back and looking forward. *Journal of Applied Psychology*, 102(3), 403.

include discussions of how to design technology using sociotechnical systems principles (Clegg, 2000); studies of how teams adapt technology to achieve their goals (Majchrzak *et al.*, 2000); and how technically oriented changes, such as lean production and integrated manufacturing, interact with work design (e.g., Dean and Snell, 1991; Parker *et al.*, 2001).

Labor relations: Keenly aware of the power differentials between employers and employees, practitioners of the labor relations approach to work focus on altering some of the contextual features of employment in the workplace. The approach recognizes trade unions as major players in the negotiation between employers and employees. It primarily addresses the *transactional* nature of work in corporate organizations and tries to get laws passed to constrain the negotiating process between the employer and the employees.

In the US, the practitioners of this approach succeeded in the passage of various US labor laws, which set the rights and duties for employees, labor unions, and employers in the US. Labor law's basic aim is to remedy the "inequality of bargaining power" between employees and employers, especially employers "organized in the corporate or other forms of ownership association." One of their signal accomplishments, the Fair Labor Standards Act (FLSA), enacted in 1938, established minimum wage, overtime pay requirements, record-keeping standards, and restrictions on child labor for most employees in the private and public sectors. It essentially guarantees workers a minimum level of compensation and protects against excessive working hours.

There have been other additions to the original FLSA, aimed at both employers and employees. For example, the Family and Medical Leave Act of 1993 creates a limited right to 12 weeks of unpaid leave in larger employers. The Employee Retirement Income Security Act of 1974 requires standards of prudent management and good governance if employers agree to provide pensions, health plans, or other benefits. The Occupational Safety and Health Act of 1970 requires employees to have a safe system of work. Under the Labor Management Reporting and Disclosure Act of 1959, labor union governance follows democratic principles. If a majority of employees in a workplace support a union, employing entities have a duty to bargain in good faith. Unions can take collective action to defend their interests, including calling their employees on strike.[10]

[10] A key source for these and other labor laws in the US is the Department of Labor. https://www.dol.gov/.

Table 2. Work design approaches.

Approach/ Characteristic	Scientific Management	Human Relations	Socio-technical Systems	Job Design	Labor Relations
Major focus	Work activities	Supervisory relations	Technical and social subsystems	Technical and social subsystems	Legal context
Objectives	Process efficiency	Human satisfaction	Joint optimization of efficiency and satisfaction	Joint optimization of efficiency and satisfaction	Context of employment
Critical assumption	Work can be scientifically studied and designed	Supervisory behavior can influence employee satisfaction	Socially cohesive groups can improve employee satisfaction	Work characteristics can be designed to improve productivity and employee satisfaction	Laws can strengthen the transactional power of employees

In Table 2, I have summarized the major differences among the approaches.

In the next section, I will discuss the futurists who have explored the linkage between work and technology, following which I will place the three major perspectives on work in context.

Futurists and the Importance of Technology

During the 1960s, triggered by fears of a rising global population, there arose a cottage industry referred to as futurism[11] to extrapolate the future from emerging trends. Futurists employed an arsenal of tools — some highly sophisticated and others mostly narrative — to paint a picture of

[11] Several prominent futurist works, such as *Limits to Growth* or *Mankind at Turning Point*, appeared in the second half of the 20th century. Organizations such as the Rand Corporation or intellectuals like Herman Kahn were also advocates of futurism.

the emerging futures. Although most futurists were focused on the big picture, some, especially those who were interested in technological change, had considered changes in work that were afoot. There were two major differences between historians and futurists. First and perhaps obviously, the context was different: the futurists were writing in the second half of the 20th century when the societal arrangements of the industrial era were giving way to what Daniel Bell[12] termed postindustrial society. Second, unlike the evidence-based presentation of historians, futurists were peering into the future and thus informed speculation was woven into their writings.

Here, I use Toffler's *Third Wave* as an example for the futurist perspective, partly because of the work's narrative simplicity but mainly because Toffler, unlike many futurists, ventured into matters pertaining to work. "The wave front analysis," he pioneered, looked at history as a succession of rolling waves of change, and focused attention on the discontinuities of history by posing the question of where the leading edge of change is taking the world. Toffler identified three waves of change: the first agricultural, the second industrial, and the third, the information age. Toffler's first wave roughly corresponds to the second stage in Lucassen's model and the second wave to Lucassen's sixth stage. Toffler was, of course, most interested in the transition from the second wave to the third, the information age. In an interpretation of Toffler, the first wave represented the age of the farmer, the second the factory worker, and the information age the clerk.[13]

In Table 3, I have summarized the pertinent differences among the three waves.

Toffler's discussion of *three* waves starts from the first, agricultural era, which was ushered in by the discovery of agriculture and enabled by tools and implements. He moves through the second industrial era brought about by non-human sources of energy and related technologies, and begins to chart out the third, the information age, triggered by the arrival of computers and Information and Computing technologies (ICT). So, in his rendition, work is confined to industrial settings. Toffler's main focus is the shift from the second to the third wave, and he deals with both the content and context of work.

---

[12]Bell, D., 1919–2011. *The Coming of Post-Industrial Society: A Venture in Social Forecasting.* New York: Basic Books, 1999.

[13]This interpretation was provided by Naisbitt in his book, *Megatrends*, published later.

Table 3. Toffler's three waves.

Wave/Characteristic of Work	First	Second	Third
Societal context	Agricultural	Industrial	Post-industrial
Location of work	Farm	Factory	Office
Sources of shift	Discovery of agriculture	Non-human energy sources	Computer revolution
Characteristics of work-focused		Content & Context	Content & Context

Toffler focused on six characteristics of both the *content* of work and the *context* of workplace in the industrial settings: Standardization, specialization, synchronization, concentration, maximization, and centralization. First, standardization of work enabled by Taylorism led to the specification of one best way to do a job. Second, specialization, or division of labor, replaced the casual jack-of-all-trades with a specialist who did only one task repetitively in the industrial age. Third, synchronization was necessitated by specialization and the use of machines: if one group of workers in a plant was late in completing a task, others down the line would also be delayed. Thus, punctuality emerged as a virtue. Fourth, industrial workplaces *concentrate* energy, population, and capital flows. Fifth, ideas such as scale efficiency led to the pursuit of maximization, and scale became an obsessive goal of major corporations. Finally, centralization of decisional power, which in Toffler's view was somewhat inevitable in industrial settings, led to *new* job titles as line and staff. Line positions focused on the core work of the organization, such as production, sales, and marketing, with line workers being directly involved in achieving the organization's primary objectives. Staff positions supported the organization by providing specialized advisory and support functions, such as human resources, accounting, legal, and public relations. Staff managers provide advice and recommendations to line managers, but do not have direct authority over them. Centralization of power also represented a shift from agricultural economies, where each locality produced its own necessities.

Toffler went on to note that many of the principles developed in the second wave, or the industrial era, have come under assault in the third wave, the information age, his primary preoccupation. Although he was less definitive about the kinds of jobs emerging in the information wave, he anticipated changes in both the context and context of work. Thus, he noted the emergence of a new job category: integrators. According to his logic, because the industrial age broke society into "thousands of interlocking parts" (p. 61), "somebody had to put things back together in a different form."[14] Those were his integrators.

Toffler surmised a world where job changes would be frequent, and the work would get increasingly less repetitive. Toffler also anticipated changes in the context of work, especially location. He anticipated the rise of telecommuting in his discussion of electronics, and foresaw a future where homes become the central hub for work, education, shopping, and other activities, enabled by advanced technology and this allows people to conduct a significant portion of their lives from home, effectively creating a "cottage industry" powered by electronics.

Work: What has Been Missing?

So far in this chapter, I have focused on three different perspectives on work — that of a historian, a management scholar, and a futurist. There have been others, e.g., religion or a sociologist. Thus, the religious aphorism "work is worship" (quoted in the first chapter) means that people should interact with God and express compassion in their work. Similarly, numerous sociologists have viewed the workplace as a location for social association. The three perspectives I have used here have all focused on the content and/or context of work, whatever meaning they have given to the term.

Characteristically, the historical approach deals with the past and provides us with an interpretive framework to understand the changes that have already taken place; the managerial approach is focused on methods of intervention to change the workplace, and the futurists are interested in speculating about the imminent changes in work. Table 4 presents a comparison of the three perspectives on three dimensions: conception of work, underlying theoretical orientation, and the driving forces in the change of work.

---

[14]Toffler, A. (1980). *The Third Wave*. Bantam Books. Toffler separated control from ownership and thus departed from Marx. According to him, integrators arose to control, but they did not own.

Table 4. A comparison of the three perspectives on work.

Perspectives on work/ Characteristics	Historical	Management	Futurist
Conception of work	Broad, includes both in and out of home	Confined to industrial settings	Confined to industrial settings
Theoretical orientation	Evolutionary (co-evolves with society)	Engineering (work can be designed for efficiency)	Predictive (characteristics of work can be anticipated)
Driving force	Societal evolution	Managerial intervention	Technology shifts

Conception of work: Lucassen's model takes the broadest view of work, and because he includes both hunter-gathering and agricultural eras in his treatise, periods before the Industrial Revolution also deal with activities that we today would consider home-related. Our view of work has shifted in the last couple of centuries, with work being confined primarily to industrial settings, with the implicit notion that the term 'work' is reserved only for activities done for wages. This is reflected in the narrower view of work that is evident in both the managerial and futurist views of work.

Theoretical orientation: Lucassen adopts an evolutionary orientation and presents the character of work as evolving along with society. Although he acknowledges the role of tools, implements, and innovation, his co-evolutionary perspective precludes strong causal assertions. Managerial perspective invokes an adaptive orientation, addressing the role of managers in fine-tuning work practices. Within the broader organization, the context and content of work can be reengineered to enhance process efficiency. The futurists' orientation is less theoretical, as they are preoccupied with anticipating changes in work.

Driving forces: Each perspective has its own views of the forces driving change in work. At the risk of repetition, historical models view work-related changes to be a mirror of societal change; the managerial perspective ascribes agency to managerial intervention, while futurists view myriad factors, especially technological change, as a driver of workplace changes.

More importantly, the three perspectives share two major assumptions:

1. *Ubiquity of work*: In spite of changes, work has always existed in societies, an occurrence that has been visible globally. Humans had to undertake diverse activities, from the hunter-gatherer era to the modern-day corporate inhabitant.
2. *Necessity of work*: Sometimes implied, the adherents of the three perspectives consider work necessary. In hunter-gathering and agricultural societies, work was necessary for food, clothing, and shelter, and as economies advanced, work patterns changed so that humans could earn wages to fulfill not only these but also other needs.

As is evident from Lucassen's work, our current conception of work is relatively new, and its origins can be traced to the industrial era that spawned it. We have come to view work as necessary and ubiquitous. Both the managerialist and futurist versions of work invoke this conception, and most of the scholarly evidence flows from this assumption. We will take this up in the next chapter.

References

Clegg, C. W. (2000). Sociotechnical principles for system design. *Applied Ergonomics*, 31, 463–477.

Cummings, T. G. (1978). Self-regulating work groups: A socio-technical synthesis. *Academy of Management Review*, 3, 625–634.

Dean, J. W. and Snell, S. A. (1991). Integrated manufacturing and job design: moderating effects of organizational inertia. *Academy of Management Journal*, 34, 776–804.

Kiggundu, M. N. (1983). Task interdependence and job design: Test of a theory. *Organizational Behavior and Human Performance*, 31, 145–172.

Lucassen, J. (2021). *The story of work: A new history of humankind.* New Haven, Connecticut: Yale University Press.

Majchrzak, A., Rice, R. E., Malhotra, A., King, N., and Ba, S. (2000). Technology adaptation: The case of a computer-supported inter-organizational virtual team. *MIS Quarterly*, 24, 569–600.

Parker, S. K., Morgeson, F., and Johns, G. (2017). 100 years of work design research: Looking back and looking forward. *Journal of Applied Psychology*, 102, 3, 403–420.

Parker, S. K., Wall, T. D., and Cordery, J. L. (2001). Future work design research and practice: Towards an elaborated model of work design. *Journal of Occupational and Organizational Psychology*, 74, 413–440.

Chapter 4

Economists and Technology

Abstract

In this chapter, I will sketch how economists have enriched our understanding of the manner in which technology has changed the workplace. In the previous two chapters, I have outlined (1) how Veblen distinguished leisure from work, and (2) how our own beliefs about work have changed over the years. As I have implied, technology has played a critical role in the transformation of work over the years, obliterating some forms of work and creating new forms. This sets the stage for the argument that technology has brought us to the threshold of non-work. Crucial to this argument is the idea that work as an activity can be automated, and one reading of technology development is as a relentless march towards automating increasingly complex levels of activity.

The construct of technology has been a continual source of awe and hostility. Techno optimists, those who cheer for technological developments, sometimes uncritically, and who have often entertained the idea that technology is a primary driver of social changes — have very often been ridiculed as technological determinists. Indeed, in an earlier chapter, I had noted that this criticism has sometimes been leveled also against Veblen. Standing in opposition to the optimists are "Luddites," a pejorative term invoked to refer to techno-pessimists. The original Luddites were members of a 19th-century movement of English textile workers who opposed the use of automated machinery due to concerns relating to worker pay and output quality.[1] Over time, the term has been used to refer to those opposed to the introduction of new technologies. The debate between the two groups — the techno-optimists and techno-pessimists — continues to this day, and its echoes can be heard in the recent warnings about the future of Artificial Intelligence.

In recent years, economic literature has identified *three* classes of technological change based on its impact on work: Technology that (1) obliterates some forms of work, (2) creates new forms of work, and (3) extends human capabilities through augmented technologies.

1. The first are *labor-destroying technologies* that obliterate some forms of work and replace workers; for example, the substitution of machines for workers in tasks where automation has a comparative advantage, as in the case of repetitive jobs taken over by robotics.
2. The second are technologies that introduce *new work*: new job tasks or job categories requiring specialized human expertise. As noted by Auto *et al.* (2023), new work typically requires expertise acquired through study, apprenticeship, or practical experience (e.g., in cosmetology, in the electrical trade), though the extent of expertise clearly varies across categories. Although not usually fundamentally different from prior work, the emergence of new work

[1]In Lancashire, new cotton spinning technologies were met with violent resistance in 1768 and 1779. These new inventions produced textiles faster and cheaper because they could be operated by less-skilled, low-wage laborers. These struggles sometimes resulted in government suppression, via Parliamentary acts, such as the Protection of Stocking Frames, etc. Act 1788. The Luddite movement began in Nottingham, England, and spread to the North West and Yorkshire between 1811 and 1816. Mill and factory owners took to shooting protesters and eventually the movement was suppressed by legal and military force, which included execution and penal transportation of accused and convicted Luddites. Malcolm L. Thomas argued in his 1970 history *The Luddites* that machine-breaking was one of the very few tactics that workers could use to increase pressure on employers, undermine lower-paid competing workers, and create solidarity among workers. These attacks on machines did not imply any necessary hostility to machinery as such; machinery was just a conveniently exposed target against which an attack could be made. Wikipedia: https://en.wikipedia.org/wiki/Luddite.

categories typically reflects the development of novel expertise within existing work activities (e.g., electrical trades skills specific to solar installations) or an increase in the market scale of a niche activity (e.g., nail care).

3. Technologies also introduce *augmentation* that potentially generates new demands for worker expertise and specialization. Augmenting technologies assist humans by providing information, insights, or tools that improve their decision-making and execution of tasks, and seamlessly integrate with current systems, minimizing disruption and facilitating a smoother transition. Examples of this type of technology across industries include:
    - *Manufacturing*: Wearable devices providing workers with real-time instructions and data on assembly lines.
    - *Healthcare*: Augmented reality systems guiding surgeons during complex procedures.
    - *Customer service*: Chatbots that assist human representatives in answering customer queries.

By enhancing existing capabilities, augmenting technology allows for incremental innovation and continuous improvement within a system. As new technologies emerge, augmenting features can be added to existing systems to keep them relevant and up-to-date. Compared to radical technological changes, augmenting technologies often require less significant training and adaptation for users, leading to a smoother transition. Because the first two categories are typically most talked about, the role of augmentation technologies and their work-related implications are often overlooked in the literature. Thus, the debate between optimists and pessimists often gets framed around the first two categories.

Before I can meaningfully examine the debate and provide some context. I address a simpler question: What has the economic scholarship to date informed us about the link between technology and work? Selective though it may be, I will outline four key ideas that we can glean from the economics literature: (1) The long-term nature of consequences of technology development; (2) Technology as a source of innovation; (3) Technology lies at the heart of economic development; and (4) How technology alters work forms.

Long-Term Consequences of Technology Development

Be it Lucassen's recent historical model or Toffler's earlier concept of waves, there has been recognition that the consequences of technology development are not confined to the short term. Indeed, Kondratieff,[2] a Russian economist, was among the first to posit a long cycle model of technology development, now called Kondratieff's cycle.

Kondratieff's theory states that the world economy experiences cycles that last 50–60 years, with alternating periods of expansion and contraction. Technological innovations are the primary drivers of the cycle. The cycles lead to new industries and increased productivity, followed by a period of consolidation and contraction. Kondratieff identified several long-term cycles that alternate between high-growth and slow-growth economic cycles. The cycles were based largely on agricultural commodities and copper prices in European countries, where he observed periods of evolution and self-correction in the different economic activities that were carried out in the domestic economies. The cycles lasted approximately 50–60 years, and they were composed of various stages that were repetitive in nature. See Box 1 for a summary of Kondratieff's first five cycles. Many economists believe that we are in a sixth Kondratieff wave that started around 2005. They primarily believe that this cycle will be fueled by advances in healthcare. Economic growth will be triggered by improved productivity in handling healthcare issues.

Kondratieff's theory has been examined by several others after him, and it has received its share of fierce criticism. The earlier critiques tended to be theoretical and originated mostly from Marxist economists. Recently, Kondratieff theory has been examined with econometric tools and has been found wanting (Metz, 2011). Like all theories of the past, newer perspectives have replaced older ones, and Kondratieff is no exception.

---

[2]Nikolai Dmitriyevich Kondratiev, also Kondratieff; (1892–1938) was a Russian Soviet economist and proponent of the New Economic Policy (NEP) best known for the business cycle theory known as Kondratiev waves. Kondratiev became an early leading figure of Soviet economics and promoted the NEP's system of small private free market enterprises in the Soviet Union. Kondratiev's theory that Western capitalist economies have long term (50 to 60 years) cycles of boom followed by depression gained recognition inside and outside the Soviet Union. Kondratiev was condemned and imprisoned in 1930, but continued to work until his execution during the Great Purge in 1938. Some of his work was published, for the first time, posthumously.

Box 1. Kondratieff's Cycles

Kondratieff's cycles include:

1. *First Cycle*: The first cycle occurred from 1780 to 1830 and was fueled by the invention of the steam engine and the growth of textile manufacturing.
2. *Second Cycle*: The second cycle (1830–1880) was triggered by the genesis of the steel industry, coinciding with the invention of the Bessemer converter.
3. *Third Cycle* (1880–1930): It occurred during the rise of electrical power. It was also the time period during which innovations in the chemical industry allowed for the mass production of commodities.
4. *Fourth Cycle* (1930–1970), fueled by the growth of the petrochemical industry. The petrochemical industry's growth also supported the growth of the auto market.
5. *Fifth Cycle*: The fifth cycle started in the 1970s, and it was triggered by the advent of computer-based information technology. The industrial society began transitioning to an information society, which turned the world into a global village.

Source: Wonglimpiyarat (2005).

So why bother? For one, Kondratieff was theorizing about technological change in the Industrial era, unlike the vastly longer canvas of human history that provided the necessary backdrop for historians like Lucassen or futurists like Toffler to build their models and theories. Predating both these intellectual streams, Kondratieff forcefully introduced the idea that technology's consequences are *long-lived* and cannot be tamed by the short-term market-oriented models prevalent in economics.

For another, and perhaps more important reason, Kondratieff shifted our perspective from linear to non-linear thinking, with his cyclical model. Technological changes come about in many ways and are not totally predictable. During the 1960s and 70s, a cottage industry had grown up with consultants calling themselves technology forecasters. That title was a misnomer as forcefully highlighted by Donald Schon (1967):

> Most technological forecasts do not forecast invention. They assume invention. In fact, they usually start with invention already introduced and go on to predict the rate or direction of diffusion. (p. 761)

It is now acknowledged that technology analysis should focus on the *futurity of present inventions* rather than predicting inventions. Thus, unlike fiction writers, empiricists — those who try to marshal evidence to bolster their conclusions — are restricted to future Implications of the current efforts and decisions.

Technology as a Source of Innovation

A second idea that has animated the economic scholarship on technology was introduced by Schumpeter. Joseph Alois Schumpeter was an Austrian political economist. Having served briefly as Finance Minister of Austria in 1919, in 1932, he emigrated to the United States to become a professor at Harvard University. Schumpeter was one of the most influential economists of the early 20th century, and popularized the term "creative destruction," a term that is used to describe the deliberate dismantling of established processes in order to make way for improved methods of production. Creative destruction is most often used to describe disruptive technologies such as railroads or, in our own time, the internet.

Schumpeter laid the foundations of what nowadays we call *corporate innovation*. Schumpeter believed that innovation is essential for economic development and wealth creation, and his writings elevated the role of entrepreneurs as the driving force behind innovation. But he argued that *large* companies are the main drivers of innovation because these companies have the capital to invest in research and development, and to deliver new products and services to customers at a lower cost. In passing, it is worth mentioning that Schumpeter's arguments fueled a line of empirical work that examined the role of R&D expenditures on profits and stock market evaluation of large firms (e.g., Hirshey, 1982; Kelm *et al.*, 1995).

Schumpeter was deferential to Kondratieff; both were not only contemporaries but shared a common theme that technological developments are ultimately good for the economy.[3] Both were writing at a time when the economic landscape was dominated by large companies of the industrial era. The empirical instances of successful startups — of the kind we have witnessed recently, such as Microsoft or Google — were not

[3]Rostow develops this theme in his historical essay, Rostow, W. W. (1975). Kondratieff, Schumpeter, and Kuznets: trend periods revisited. *The Journal of Economic History*, 35(4), 719–753.

available to them. Among the many ideas underpinning their writings, two are relevant to the thesis of this book: that technological change is disruptive, *it destroys existing order for the betterment of society, and secondly, that by disrupting processes, they significantly impact the work activities in a corporation.*

Technology and Economic Development

For most of the first half of the 20th century, economists had framed economic growth mainly in terms of capital and labor, and technology did not feature as a major driver. This situation changed with Robert Solow,[4] who highlighted the importance of technological progress as a key driver of economic growth.

Solow developed a model of economic growth by considering factors like labor and capital, but initially treated technological change as an *exogenous* factor influencing the production function.[5] The production function is one of the key concepts of mainstream neoclassical economic theories, specifying the relation between quantities of physical inputs and quantities of output of goods. Through his analysis, Solow showed that a substantial part of economic growth is not accounted for by increased labor or capital inputs, and he attributed this to technological innovation,

---

[4]Robert Solow is a Nobel Prize-winning economist best known for the Solow Growth Model, which highlighted the role of technological progress in long-term economic growth. His work reshaped modern macroeconomic theory.

[5]Generative AI Produced the following: A production function is a mathematical model that shows how the physical output of a production process relates to its physical inputs. It's used in economics to measure the efficiency of production and to help businesses decide how much to produce and what combination of inputs to use. Here are some key points about production functions: *Inputs and outputs*: A production function relates the quantity of physical inputs to the quantity of output. Inputs can include land, labor, capital, and entrepreneurship; *Efficiency*: A production function measures how efficiently a business is producing goods or services; *Decision making*: Businesses use production functions to decide how much to produce and what combination of inputs to use. For example, a manufacturing company might use a production function to determine the best combination of labor and capital to produce a certain amount of output; *Diminishing returns to scale*: At high levels of production, marginal costs usually increase. This is known as diminishing returns to scale, which means that increasing the quantity of inputs doesn't increase the quantity of output in proportion.

now known as the "Solow residual." Solow's work emphasized the importance of fostering technological advancements to achieve sustained economic growth, influencing policies related to research and development (R&D) investment by governments.

Although subsequent work refined Solow's analysis, it did little to upset the basic conclusion that capital accumulation provides a very incomplete explanation for why countries grow (Eaton and Kortum, 2005). It is now well recognized that technology lies at the heart of economic development. There are several ways in which technology creates technological progress: First, and obviously, technology has been a major driver of economic growth, creating millions of jobs, improving the quality of life, and increasing productivity. Second, it has improved efficiency in existing industries, allowing companies to remain competitive. Third, it has led to the creation of new industries and products, such as e-commerce. Fourth, it has created new growth opportunities, such as the digital economy, which fosters new markets and collaboration. Fifth, it has enhanced communication and remote work. Finally, it helps different global regions grow by diffusing new technologies.

Techno-optimists cheer the relentless march of technology and economic progress, but both Kondratieff and Schumpeter had earlier alerted us to some probable unwelcome outcomes associated with technological change. Indeed, technological change may impose some real costs on individuals: Some jobs would become obsolete, although some new forms of work might come into existence. For the theme of this book, this is an important idea, and economic scholarship has tracked the link between technology and employment, a topic I touch upon in the next section.

Technology and Work

Economists' research has documented three major facets of the influence of technology on labor: (1) Effect of technological change at the macro level; (2) The differences in the impacts of technology on labor; and (3) The shift in skill sets created by technological change.

Unlike the popular fears (e.g., those stoked by Luddites) about job losses due to technology, macroeconomic research — economic research that tracks the influence of technology at the level of economy as a whole — has concluded that although many technologies are designed to save labor by replacing human workers by machinery, *to date* at the aggregate level, there is *little* evidence that technological change has led to widespread unemployment over the centuries.

According to some economic theory, several compensating mechanisms can counterbalance the initial labor-saving impact of new technologies (e.g., Hötte *et al.*, 2023; Acemoglu and Restrepo, 2019; Baldwin *et al.*, 2019; Vivarelli, 2014). First, technological change can increase the demand for labor by creating *new* tasks and jobs that are directly associated with the new technology. This idea has led to the concept of augmenting technologies, a topic that I will deal with in the next section. Second, if automation increases productivity, it releases production resources, which can raise the demand for labor in non-automated tasks within the same firm or industry. Third, technology can also increase the demand for labor through the demand for goods and services that are produced when new technologies boost productivity growth and lead to lower production costs and consumer prices (Bessen, 2020).

Economists have acknowledged that the influence of technology on jobs is not uniform. For one, technological change that leads to new products generally tends to increase demand for labor, where process technologies have mixed results. The employment effects of the latter have been mostly favorable for non-production workers, high-skill labor, and service jobs (Krüger, 2008; Syrquin, 2012). For another, it takes time to observe the effect of technology on labor: When new technology appears, newer tasks have to evolve to take advantage of the benefits of the new technology, and this takes time.

Economic research has also documented that technological change alters the demand for skill sets in the economy:

1. Low-skill, production, and manufacturing workers have been *adversely* affected by technological change over the last decades.
2. Many occupations in the lower end but also in the middle part of the skill distribution will continue to evolve and demand a changing set of skills due to technological progress.
3. Some workers who experience job loss might *not* be able to engage in upskilling or make the transition to new jobs.

It is now recognized that the influence of technological change on labor varies across sectors. In particular, the introduction of robotics has generally been unfavorable to low-skilled workers in blue-collar occupations (Acemoglu and Restrepo, 2020; Blanas, 2019; Edler and

Ribakova, 1994; Faber, 2020; Graetz and Michaels, 2018; Jung and Lim, 2020), as well as routine manual occupations (Acemoglu and Restrepo, 2020). By contrast, information and communication technologies (ICT) have generally been favorable to highly skilled workers.

I would note that the economic views have oscillated between two extremes: One view is that technology will bring less work, make workers redundant, or end work by replacing workers. The other major view is that technology will create abundant opportunities for workers and boost economies. More importantly, the evidence on which the conclusions are based, by necessity, is historical and does not take into account the possible changes on the horizon. In an opinion piece, two scholars advanced a carefully constructed opinion in a Broking Institution[6] paper (Howard & Schultz, 2019):

> Historically, as technology has changed the way work is done, the number of jobs created has outstripped the number of jobs eliminated. There is concern that although history may be correct, the future may reverse history, and worker displacement and unemployment due to automation, AI, and robotics will be widespread (Ford, 2015). However, future forecasting is difficult and complicated. If analysts in 1870 in the United States had been informed that agriculture sector employment would go from almost 50% of the workforce to less than 2% in 2018, they also would be hard-pressed to foretell a burgeoning health care sector, software, and services as major sources of employment (Autor, 2018; Daly, 1981; Segal, 2018). Still, with current evidence of technological displacement, there is a growing preponderance of analysis and commentary supporting the occurrence of technologically induced unemployment. (Brynjolfsson and McAfee, 2014; Frey and Osborne, 2013)

I quote the two Brookings scholars at length not only to underscore the difficulty of predicting the influence of technological change, especially on work but also, perhaps more importantly, to underscore the challenges of the new technologies. Automation has been gathering momentum in the last few decades, and the twin technological changes — robotics

---

[6]The Brookings Institution is a leading American think tank based in Washington, D.C., known for its research on economics, governance, and public policy. It has played a significant role in shaping policy debates since its founding in 1916.

and digitization — have dramatically affected the industrial landscape. I will spotlight automation in the next two chapters.

References

Acemoglu, D. and Restrepo, P. (2019). Automation and new tasks: How technology displaces and reinstates labor. *Journal of Economic Perspectives*, 33(2), 3–30.

Acemoglu, D. and Restrepo, P. (2020). Robots and jobs: Evidence from US labor markets. *Journal of Political Economy*, 128(6), 2188–2244.

Autor, D. H., Levy, F., and Murnane, R. J. (2003). The skill content of recent technological change: An empirical exploration. *The Quarterly Journal of Economics*, 118(4), 1279–1333.

Baldwin, R. (2019). *The Globotics Upheaval: Globalization, Robotics, and the Future of Work*. Oxford: Oxford University Press.

Bessen, J. (2020). Information technology and industry concentration. *Journal of Law & Economics*, 63(3), 531.

Blanas, S. (2019). The distinct effects of information technologies and communication technologies on skill demand. *Industrial Relations: A Journal of Economy and Society*, 63(4), 442–490.

Brynjolfsson, E, McAfee, A. (2014). The second machine age: work, progress and prosperity in a time of brilliant technologies.

Daly, P. A. (1981). Agriculture Employment: Has the decline ended. Monthly Labor Review.

Eaton, J. and Kortum, S. (2005). Technology in the global economy: A framework for quantitative analysis. Unpublished manuscript.

Edler, D. and Ribakova, T. (1994). The impact of industrial robots on the level and structure of employment in Germany — A simulation study for the period 1980–2000. *Technological Forecasting and Social Change*, 45(3), 255–274.

Faber, M. (2020). Robots and reshoring: Evidence from Mexican labor markets. *Journal of International Economics*, 127, 103384.

Frey, C. B. and Osborne, M. A. (2013). The future of employment: How susceptibility are jobs to computerization? (Oxford: Oxford Martin School, University of Oxford).

Ford, M. (2015). The rise of the robots. Basic Books, New York.

Graetz, G. and Michaels, G. (2018). Robots at work. *Review of Economics and Statistics*, 100(5), 753–768.

Hirshey, M. (1982). Intangible capital aspects of advertising and R&D expenditures. *The Journal of Industrial Economics*, 30(4), 375–390.

Hötte, K., Somers, M., and Theodorakopoulos, A. (2023). Technology and jobs: A systematic literature review. *Technological Forecasting and Social Change*, 194, 122750.

Howard, J. and Schulte, P. (2019). The impact of technology on work and the workforce.

Jung, J. H. and Lim, D. G. (2020). Industrial robots, employment growth, and labor cost: A simultaneous equation analysis. *Technological Forecasting and Social Change*, 159, 120202.

Kelm, K. M., Narayanan, V. K., and Pinches, G. E. (1995). The response of capital markets to the R&D process. *Technological Forecasting and Social Change*, 49(1), 75–88.

Krüger, J. J. (2008). Productivity and structural change: A review of the literature. *Journal of Economic Surveys*, 22(2), 330–363.

Metz, R. (2011). Do Kondratieff waves exist? How time series techniques can help to solve the problem. *Cliometrica*, 5(3), 205–238.

Schon, D. A. (1967). Forecasting and technological forecasting. *Daedalus*, 759–770.

Segal, M. (2018). Automatic pilots: Automation is set to change your job not take it away. 563, S132–S135.

Syrquin, M. (2012). Two approaches to the study of structural change and economic development: Kuznets and Pasinetti. *Structural Dynamics and Economic Growth*, 1(2), 69–87.

Vivarelli, M. (2014). Innovation, employment and skills in advanced and developing countries: A survey of economic literature. *Journal of Economic Issues*, 48(1), 123–154.

Wonglimpiyarat, J. (2005). The nano-revolution of Schumpeter's Kondratieff cycle. *Technovation*, 25(11), 1349–1354.

Chapter 5

Automation and Work

Abstract

It has become obvious that automation changes work in an organization, both the needed set of activities and the skill sets required of humans in the organization. Automation itself is complex, and during the last three decades, we have witnessed three waves of automation: roboticization, digitalization, and, most recently, Artificial Intelligence (AI). These different technological advances influence different types of work in an organization. In this chapter, I focus on roboticization and digitalization, and in the next, AI. The reasons for dealing with AI separately are two-fold: first, the scholarly evidence is much firmer for the first two types of automation, given their longer history, whereas AI adoption in organizations is too recent to have generated good data, and second, a mushrooming stream of literature has focused on the consequences of AI, beyond its impact on work.

Recall that in the second chapter, I advanced a view of work as activities undertaken by individuals out of necessity, transactional, and conducted within an industrial setting. Definitionally, I have narrowed the perspective on work to the activities conducted within an organization; therefore, technology shifts, and the changes in work activities; thus, provoked have major consequences for the organization. Using the logic that the consequences are contingent on the type of technology, that is, different technologies affect different activities, I suggest that different types of automation are consequential for different aspects of an organization, both activities and skill sets.

To portray automation itself as complex, I put forth three successive waves in the recent history of automation: roboticization, digitalization, and Artificial Intelligence (AI). Although AI can be viewed as belonging to the wave of digitalization, I treat it separately because of the hype, hopes, and fears associated with AI in the public consciousness. Moreover, scholarly data, especially from economists, is more definitive with respect to the first two waves of automation, whereas firm conclusions about AI's impact on work wait for good evidence.

The scheme of this chapter is as follows: First, I will sketch the three major facets of automation: robotization and digitization that have buffeted organizations in recent years, and the newest arrival, AI. In doing so, I am extending to the present day the story of technological change that both historians, such as Lucassen, and futurists, such as Toffler, outlined. Second, I will employ the model of organizations originally proposed by Talcott Parsons to characterize the influence of technology on organizations.

The Role of Automation

It is unlikely that Veblen, Lucassen, or Toffler could have predicted the magnitude of change that has happened in the world, and especially in the US, since their writing. Yet the last few decades have witnessed significant changes in society, mainly due to technological innovation, with many more things in the offing. These innovations have occurred in both information and communication technologies (ICT) and other fields such as neural, biological, and physical sciences. In drawing out the linkage between technological change and work, I will focus primarily on automation.

Automation is the use of technology to perform activities with minimal human intervention. It can involve using machines, robotics, or computer programs to carry out processes, control machinery, or manage data (IBM, 2025). I will focus on two major sources of automation that have benefited organizations in their pursuit of productivity and customer satisfaction: robotics and digitalization. Although I will deal with them separately, innovations involve mixing and matching these and other technologies. This technological confluence is acknowledged in Figure 1.

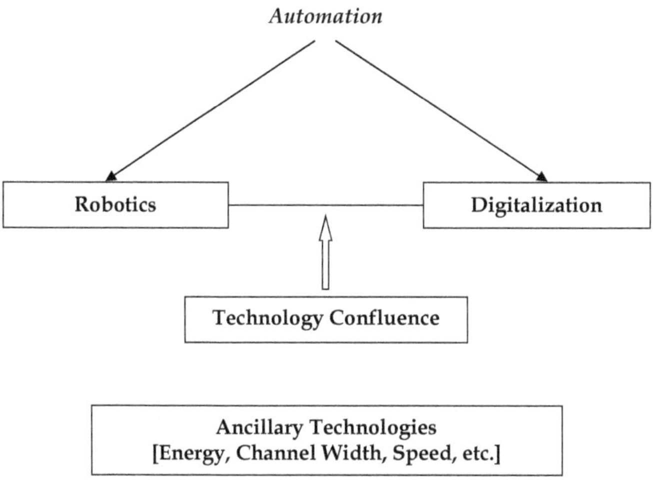

Fig. 1. A schematic of automation.

As shown in the figure, automation is founded on the twin pillars of robotization and digitalization — but they leverage each other when necessary. For example, robotics heavily relies on digital computing as the "brain" behind robot actions. Complex algorithms and data processing enable robots to perceive their environment, make decisions, and execute movements with precision. Indeed, some have opined that modern robots are essentially physical manifestations of digital computations, allowing them to perform tasks.

In addition, both robotics and digitalization depend on what I have labeled *ancillary technologies* — technologies that supports the primary operations of another focal technology. These include (but are not limited to) new sources of power, modes of communication, analysis tools, or visualization. For example:

(1) Hydrogen power or the generation of electricity by using hydrogen fuel in a fuel cell, a clean energy that can be used to power vehicles, and generate electricity for home.
(2) 6G, the sixth generation of cellular networks, expected to be available in early 2030, which will offer faster data speeds and more reliable connections than previous generations.
(3) Quantum computing, a field that uses quantum mechanics to solve complex problems faster than classical computers.

(4) Virtual reality (VR) or the use of computer modeling and simulation that enables a person to interact with an artificial three-dimensional (3D) visual sensory environment.

While acknowledging that developments in ancillary technologies and their applications will substantially impact automation, I will restrict my focus to robotization and digitization, primarily to develop the implications for work.

Roboticization

Robots are machines that can do work previously done by human beings. According to the *Cambridge English Dictionary*, robotization is "the act or process of introducing robots (machines controlled by computers) to do work that was previously done by people." It is thus a facet of automation, which as we have noted before, is the use of technology to perform tasks with minimal human intervention. Robots are usually designed to mimic the movements of a human worker and repeat them endlessly; indeed, they can perform basic and repetitive tasks more efficiently and accurately than humans.

Robots are now everywhere in our lives. They are used in households; for example, after COVID-19 broke out, there was an upsurge in the sale of robotic vacuum cleaners. Educational robots are used in educational settings to facilitate interactive learning experiences. Medical robots are used in hospitals, surgeries, and ambulances to perform tasks like assisting surgeons or conducting entire surgeries. It is reported that as early as 2007, a great number of robot-assisted minimally invasive surgeries were performed worldwide. Industrial robots are used in factories and warehouses on assembly lines across all types of industries, handling jobs that range from loading materials to welding parts (Orient Software, 2022). Agricultural robots are used to perform tasks like planting, harvesting, and pest control.

Historical evolution: Although historians have traced the idea of roboticization several centuries before, one could say that by the arrival of programmable computers in the 1940s, the first real robots began to take shape (Daftdar, 2023). In the 1950s, George Devol[1] invented and patented a reprogrammable manipulator (basically a robot) called Unimate, which

[1] George Devol was the inventor of the first industrial robot, Unimate, in the 1950s. His innovations laid the foundation for modern automation in manufacturing.

in the 1960s was bought by Joseph Engleberger, who modified it into an industrial robot. It was a programmable robotic arm that was installed seven years later, on the assembly line of New Jersey General Motors. For his efforts and success, Engleberger is known in the industry as "the Father of Robotics."

In 1966, the Stanford Research Institute[2] created Shakey, the first general-purpose mobile robot able to reason concerning its own actions. While other robots would have to be instructed on each individual step in order to complete a larger task, Shakey could analyze commands and break them down into basic chunks by itself. These actions involved traveling from one location to another, turning light switches on and off, opening and closing the doors, climbing up and down from rigid objects, and pushing movable objects around. Three years later, Victor Scheinman[3] created Stanford Arm, which became standard for the design of future robot arms. In 1985, the first robot, called Puma350, was used in the medical field for surgery. Its purpose was to orient a needle for a brain biopsy under computerized tomography guidance. It was discontinued later due to safety issues (Daftdar, 2023).

With further advancements in technology, robots started becoming more and more autonomous. In 2002, a batch of SDR-4C robots was introduced, which remembered people's faces, danced to disco, and even sang in harmony. In 2015, Nanyang Technological University created Nadine, the most human-like robot ever made. It currently operates as a university receptionist. Some scientists and engineers even hold the belief that space colonization, which they find inevitable, will be fully automated because humans cannot survive extended periods of time in outer space (Campa *et al.*, 2019).

Uses and applications of robotics: Robotics has been introduced to conduct repetitive tasks, including:

1. **To handle a continually expanding range of materials, primarily stable or hazardous:** This technique also reduces the risks of injury to human employees because robots never become weary.

---

[2] Stanford Research Institute (SRI) International, formerly part of Stanford University, has been a hub for breakthrough innovations in robotics, computing, and artificial intelligence. It played a key role in early internet and AI developments.

[3] In the 1960s, Victor Scheinman developed the Stanford Arm, one of the first electrically powered, computer-controlled robotic arms. It was a milestone in programmable robotics.

2. **For picking, packing, and palletizing:** After the product has been constructed, robots quickly choose individual parts, pack them appropriately, and palletize them.
3. **For part transfer:** Part transfer robots provide a secure way to keep employees out of dangerous situations and injury-free.
4. **For machine loading:** Robots that load and unload machinery are used in manufacturing line tasks involving the loading and unloading of parts.
5. **For assembly:** Putting together product pieces takes a lot of time and effort, and mistakes in judgment, boredom, and other uncontrolled variables can easily derail the process.
6. **For welding:** Heat and pressure are used to connect metal components, which is a risky operation that demands flawless accuracy.
7. **For painting:** Industrial paint robots are generally used in the automobile sector to uniformly paint components and equipment without leaving paint drips or markings.
8. **For dispensing:** Dispensing robots are positioned in a strategic location close to the product route for procedures that call for the application of glue, paint, or spray to a surface.
9. **Processing:** Before being made available, some items must go through a particular form of processing, such as carving, polishing, or sawing (Universal Robots, 2022).

Roboticization brings numerous benefits to organizations. They can reduce costs and human error; they can improve employee engagement; they can be flexible, simple, and fast to implement, and help reduce worker shortages. It is therefore no surprise that many firms have decided to bring roboticization to their organization. The experiences of the manufacturing, pharmaceutical, and aerospace industries are illustrative.

> In *automotive* factories, robots have become commonplace tools. By one estimate, the automotive industry had become the largest user of robots worldwide in 2020. In construction, robots can be used to automate industrial construction projects (Deveraj *et al.*, 2025).
>
> In the *pharmaceutical* industry, robots have been well-suited for assembly work and drug discovery tasks because they protect the integrity of pharmaceutical products and the health of employees. Robots are also used in pharmaceutical research, with processes such as sample

> preparation done by a robotic arm for nuclear magnetic resonance (Sadiku *et al.*, 2018).
>
> The *aerospace* industry uses robots for a growing range of tasks, but in contrast to the automotive sector, their use is far more recent and limited; likewise, robotic technologies are increasingly being used by the space sector. For example, Boeing has installed a robotic system at its Everett plant in Washington State to drill and rivet fuselage sections of the 777 airliner. Located close to the Boeing Everett plant, Electroimpact, one of the world's largest aircraft assembly line integrators, has been using robots for drilling and fastening since 2001. Kuka is responsible for integrating robotic drilling stations into Northrop Grumman's F-35 Lightning II. Robotic solutions are increasingly being used to conduct dimensional checks and visual inspection testing (Bogue, 2018).

Needless to say, roboticization has fundamentally changed the way many organizations operate. In Figure 2, I have reproduced photographs of automotive factories before and after robotics came to dominate automobile production.

As is easily noticeable, the modern-day roboticized shop floor needs relatively *very few* workers. A similar observation can be made in the case of warehousing — for example, Amazon — chemical plants, aerospace, electricals, and many other industries, where roboticization has been introduced. But before I touch upon the impact of robotics on work, let me focus on the role of digitalization, the second component of automation.

Fig. 2. How Robotics has Changed Automobile Manufacturing.

Digitalization

During the last few years, there has been significant overlap in the use of two terms, digitization and digitalization. Following Gradillas and Thomas (2025), I distinguish between digitization and digitalization. Digitization is the process of converting information from an analog format to a digital format, and this can include converting physical objects, documents, images, sounds, or signals into digital representations.

In Figure 3, I have displayed pictures before and after the use of digital photography.

As indicated by the figure, by 2005, consumers had become accustomed to and indeed started demanding the use of digital instead of older technologies, partly because of the enhanced convenience and also because digital photographs enabled easier transmission. I hasten to point out that this shift to a digital world has not come about easily: For example, Kodak,[4] once a blue-chip US company, fell from grace in the wake of digitization.

Unlike digitization, *digitalization* is used to connote the transformation of the business environment: This definition encompasses organizational application, new business opportunities, economic transformation, and the new socioeconomic reality. Business transformation refers to the

Fig. 3. Digitization in front of Vatican.

[4]Kodak was once a dominant American photography company, known for its film products and consumer cameras. However, its failure to adapt to the rise of digital photography led to its decline and bankruptcy in 2012, often cited as a cautionary tale in innovation management.

broader economic and social context (e.g., Busch *et al.*, 2018; Fuentes *et al.*, 2019; Whelan *et al.*, 2013).

Evolution of digitalization: The adoption of Information and Computing technologies (ICTs) marked the first stage in digitalization. Although historians may look back on the abacus as one of the starting points of human efforts to automate computation, Alan Turing[5] is typically credited as the father of modern computing by most technologists. He was famous for his work decoding the encryption of German Enigma machines during the Second World War, and detailing a procedure known as the Turing Test. Alan Turing's theoretical work on the Turing machine inspired the design of ENIAC, the first general-purpose electronic computer. ENIAC was made of vacuum tubes, with punch cards used for data entry.

The march toward digitalization was characterized by technological innovations that were initially powered by the thirst for power and speed. As Gordon Moore, a co-founder of Intel, observed in 1965, data show that computer processing speeds roughly double every two years. Technology companies used this observation, now known as "Moore's Law," in their planning, and computers have since evolved through several generations, each characterized by new technology, with the second generation using transistors instead of vacuum tubes, the third generation using integrated circuits, and the fourth generation using microprocessors. Over the course of its evolution, computers became smaller, decentralized, more powerful, and faster. Aided by many ancillary technologies, later innovations extended the functionality of computing technology.

ICTs have affected the functioning of the organizations in many ways:

1. They enable automating repetitive tasks, streamlined workflows, and reduced manual errors through systems like Enterprise Resource Planning (ERP).
2. ICTs facilitate seamless communication between employees, teams, and stakeholders through email, instant messaging, and video conferencing.

[5] Alan Turing was a British mathematician and computer scientist who is considered one of the fathers of modern computing. His work on the Turing Machine and codebreaking during World War II laid foundational concepts for artificial intelligence and cryptography.

3. Access to real-time data through ICT enables organizations to analyze trends, identify patterns, and make data-driven decisions to optimize operations and strategies.
4. ICTs enable businesses to manage customer interactions effectively, improving customer service, personalization, and loyalty.
5. ICTs enable organizations to operate across geographical boundaries, accessing new markets and customer bases through online platforms.

During the 1970s, hardware evolution dominated, with IBM being the undisputed leader. The 1980s witnessed a shift from *hardware to software*. This shift also enabled more widespread *personal* use of computers. Microsoft became the computing frontline leader by giving ordinary people tools like word processing. During the 1990s, the World Wide Web turned Internet URLs into website names that people could read. Google, which offered the ultimate personal service, free access to the vast public library of the Internet, and soon everyone's gateway to the web, became the new computing leader. In the 2000s, computing evolved yet again to become a *social* medium as well as a personal tool. So now Facebook challenged Google, as Google challenged Microsoft, and as Microsoft challenged IBM.

Recently, *digitization* — the technical process of the creation of digital artifacts through conversion, representation, and enhancement — made it possible to tap data and information that were not numerical and subject them to analysis and business applications. Digital artifacts include the conversion of analog or physical precursors into digital form, such as paper being scanned into an image. Digitization also embraces the representation of real-world phenomena in digital form, such as digital topographic models of the earth, and the enhancement of analog or physical artifacts, such as placing sensors on physical objects. Still later, the evolution of digitalization has been facilitated by newer digital technologies, including cloud computing, machine learning, Internet of Things (IoT), and business intelligence.[6]

[6] The *cloud* is a metaphor for a global computing network of remote servers that run applications, store data, and deliver content and services. The cloud enables data to be accessed online from internet-enabled devices, rather than solely from local computers. *Machine learning* (ML) is a branch of Artificial Intelligence (AI) focused on enabling computers and machines to imitate the way that humans learn, to perform tasks autonomously, and to improve their performance and accuracy through experience and exposure to more data

Impact of Automation on Employment

The introduction of robotics and ICTs has had a major impact on organizations. One of the most significant impacts of robotization on blue-collar jobs has been the automation of many tasks that were previously done manually. Automation has been instrumental in increasing efficiency and reducing costs, but it has also resulted in a reduction in the number of workers required to perform certain tasks. As illustrated in Figure 1, showcasing the shifts on the shop floor, machines have replaced human workers in many manufacturing plants, leading to a decline in the number of jobs available in this field (Standby Personnel, 2025). During the 1980s and beyond, cost reductions made possible by ICTs partly caused firms to undertake corporate restructuring — often a euphemism for layoff. ICT adoption has also led to what is called 'delayering' or removing layers of management.[7] In what follows, I will provide an overview of the consequences of automation on jobs.

The available evidence from scholarly literature suggests that automation affects types of work activities and employment levels (see also Filippi *et al.*, 2023).

Work activities: Automation substitutes for human, physical work, or operating machinery in a *predictable* (i.e., highly structured) environment, data processing, and data collection (Chui *et al.*, 2016; Manyika, 2017).

(https://www.ibm.com/think/topics/machine-learning#:~:text=Machine%20learning%20(ML)%20is%20a,and%20exposure%20to%20more%20data.) *The Internet of Things* (IoT) is a network of physical objects that are connected to the internet and can communicate with each other. IoT devices, also called "smart objects," use sensors to collect data and perform tasks. *Business intelligence* (BI) is a process that uses data to help organizations make decisions. BI tools analyze historical and current data to help businesses understand their current state and make data-driven decisions.

[7]Delayering means the reduction of the number of management levels in an organization, i.e., the flattening of an organization's hierarchy. However, it should not be confused with other related concepts of corporate restructuring, such as downsizing or decentralization (Littler *et al.*, 2003; Rajan and Wulf, 2006). Downsizing basically means workforce reduction. If certain management levels are targeted, this can lead to delayering. Decentralization means the delegation of decision-making authority to lower management levels. If decision power of wiped-out managerial positions is relocated down the hierarchy, delayering would indeed imply more decentralization (Rajan and Wulf, 2006).

Kuhn, D. (2011). *Delayering and Firm Performance: Evidence From Swiss Firm-Level Data* (No. 2011/02). WWZ discussion paper.

These activities are frequent in the manufacturing, accommodation and food service, and retail trade sectors (Manyika, 2017). Indeed, it is estimated that 45% of the work activities that workers perform can be automated by adapting existing technologies, and an additional 13% could be automated if the technologies designed to understand natural language reached a median level of human performance (Chui *et al.*, 2015).

Employment: According to some studies, industrial robots decrease the routine employment share, while they increase the share of non-routine analytic or manual occupations (Webb, 2019), other studies suggest that industrial robots lead to a reduction in the number of managers in the firm, but the number of non-managerial workers increases (Dixon *et al.*, 2019, 2021). Software mainly affects occupations that involve information processing based on pre-defined rules; on the contrary, occupations that require interpersonal and manual skills are not impacted (Webb, 2019). Occupations that are most exposed to automation technologies include office and administrative support, production, and delivery occupations; instead, the least exposed occupations are those in healthcare, management, architecture and engineering, academia, and art. In general, low- and medium-skilled occupations are declining, while high-skill occupations are increasing; however, even some low- and medium-skilled occupations are growing (Vermeulen *et al.*, 2018).

In a very recent study from MIT, the authors (Autor *et al.*, 2003) conclude:

1. About 60% of jobs in the US represent new types of work, which have been created since 1940.
2. The negative effects of automation on employment were more than twice as great in the 1980–2018 period as in the 1940–1980 period. There was a more modest and positive change in the effect of augmentation on employment in 1980–2018, as compared to 1940–1980.[8]

---

[8]To quote: A century ago, that computer programmer may have been working on a farm. From about 1940 through 1980, for instance, jobs like elevator operator and typesetter tended to get automated. But at the same time, more workers filled roles such as shipping and receiving clerks, buyers and department heads, and civil and aeronautical engineers, where technology created a need for more employees. From 1980 through 2018, the ranks of cabinetmakers and machinists, among others, have been thinned by automation, while, for instance, industrial engineers, and operations and systems researchers and analysts have enjoyed growth.

The data on automation does not show that automation has reduced the total employment, but rather it has shifted the required labor force to a higher level of expertise. Today, however, we are witnessing the next stage in digitalization, the development and diffusion of AI that is typically portrayed as a game-changer. Given its recency, I will deal with the challenge of AI in a separate (following) chapter.

References

Autor, D. H., Levy, F., and Murnane, R. J. (2003). The skill content of recent technological change: An empirical exploration. *The Quarterly Journal of Economics*, 118(4), 1279–1333.

Bogue, R. (2018). The growing use of robots by the aerospace industry. *Industrial Robot: An International Journal*, 45(6), 705–709.

Busch, P. A., Henriksen, H. Z., and Saebo, O. (2018). Opportunities and challenges of digitized discretionary practices: A public service worker perspective. *Government Information Quarterly*, 35(4): 547–556. https://doi.org/10.1016/j.giq.2018.09.003.

Campa, R., Szocik, K., and Braddock, M. (2019). Why space colonization will be fully automated. *Technological Forecasting and Social Change*, 143, 162–171.

Chui, M., Manyika, J., and Miremadi, M. (2016). Where machines could replace humans—and where they can't (yet). *McKinsey Quarterly*, 30(2), 1–9.

Daftdar. (2023). History and evolution of robots. Science ABC. Available at: https://www.scienceabc.com/innovation/history-evolution-robots-robotics-pathfinder-hal-nadine.html [Accessed 15 October 2025].

Devaraj, E., Kakaravada, I., and Kumar, N. (2025). Robotics, automation, and artificial intelligence's future in the automotive sector. In *Integrating Intelligent Control Systems with Sensor Technologies*. Hershey, PA: IGI Global Scientific Publishing, pp. 281–310.

Dixon, J., Hong, B., and Wu, L. (2019). The employment consequences of robots: Firm-level evidence. SSRN Electronic Journal. https://doi.org/10.2139/ssrn.3422581.

Dixon, J., Hong, B., and Wu, L. (2021). The robot revolution: Managerial and employment consequences for firms. *Management Science*, 67(9), 5586–5605. https://doi.org/10.1287/mnsc.2020.3812.

Filippi, E., Banno, M., and Trento, S. (2023). Automation technologies and their impact on employment: A review, synthesis and future research agenda. *Technological Forecasting and Social Change*, 191, 122448.

Fuentes, C., Hagberg, J., and Kjellberg, H. (2019). Soundtracking: Music listening practices in the digital age. *European Journal of Marketing*, 53(3), 483–503. https://doi.org/10.1108/ejm-10-2017-0753.

Gradillas, M. and Thomas, L. D. (2025). Distinguishing digitization and digitalization: A systematic review and conceptual framework. *Journal of Product Innovation Management*.

IBM. (2025). What is automation? IBM Think. Available at: https://www.ibm.com/think/topics/automation [Accessed 15 October 2025].

Littler, C. R., Wiesner, R., and Dunford, R. (2003). The dynamics of delayering: Changing management structures in three countries. *Journal of management Studies*, 40(2), 225–256.

Manyika, J. (2017). A future that works: AI, automation, employment, and productivity. Technical Report No. 60, McKinsey Global Institute.

Orient Software. (2022). Robots in everyday life. Available at: https://www.orientsoftware.com/blog/robots-in-everyday-life/ [Accessed 15 October 2025].

Rajan, R. G. and Wulf, J. (2006). The flattening firm: Evidence from panel data on the changing nature of corporate hierarchies. *The Review of Economics and Statistics*, 88(4), 759–773.

Sadiku, M. and Musa, M. (2018). Robots in the chemical industry. *Invention Journal of Research Technology in Engineering & Management*, 2(1), 21–23.

Standby Personnel. (2025). The impact of technology on blue-collar jobs: Preparing for the future. Available at: https://www.standbypersonnel.com/blog/health-nutrition/the-impact-of-technology-on-blue-collar-jobs-preparing-for-the-future [Accessed 15 October 2025].

Universal Robots. (2022). https://www.universal-robots.com/in/blog/impact-of-robotics.

Vermeulen, J., Kesselhut, A., Pyka, P., and Saviotti, P. (2018). The impact of automation on employment: Just the usual structural change? *Sustainability*, 10(5), 1661. https://doi.org/10.3390/su10051661.

Webb, M. (2019). The impact of artificial intelligence on the labor market. *SSRN Electronic Journal*. https://doi.org/10.2139/ssrn.3482150.

Whelan, E., Golden, W. and Donnellan, B. (2013). Digitising the R&D social network: Revisiting the technological gatekeeper. *Information Systems Journal*, 23(3), 197–218. https://doi.org/10.1111/j.1365-2575.2011.00384.x.

Chapter 6

Artificial Intelligence (AI): The Next Chapter in Automation

Abstract

I continue with the story of automation by outlining the evolution of Artificial Intelligence (AI) and its potential impact on organizations. AI has created so much hype recently, but in spite of its evolving technological details, its impact on work and, in general, the social systems in which we are embedded are still being debated. I present AI as another chapter in the evolving saga of automation.

The most recent arrival in the evolution of digitalization is Artificial Intelligence (AI). "AI is a broad field that encompasses many different disciplines, including computer science, data analytics and statistics, hardware and software engineering, linguistics, neuroscience, and even philosophy and psychology."[1] AI is being implemented in organizations, and hence its evolution in recent times has focused on applications. New variants of ChatGPT and other modifications are continually arriving at the doorstep of users.

Therefore, this is a story *in progress*.

The excitement created by AI is not merely because of its recency but also because of the hype and the fears that it has generated. We can parse the hype into four major clusters: investments, startups, sectors affected, and tools and technologies.

---

[1] https://cloud.google.com/learn/what-is-artificial-intelligence.

1. In recent years, AI has attracted significant investment in the private sector, with the US leading both China and Europe. One estimate puts US investment at over 300 billion and China at 132 billion; Europe has announced that it would mobilize €200 billion for investment in AI.[2,3]
2. The AI-based *startups* have been able to muster lots of attention. Thus, by 2019, Forbes started publishing the top 50 AI companies of the year.[4]
3. Almost all sectors are expected to be affected by AI — Healthcare, Retail, Transportation, Marketing, Banking and finance, Customer service, Manufacturing, Administrative work, Legal services, Entertainment — to name a few. The excitement of AI has even spilled over to education, as seen in the words of Salman Khan:

> We are at a turning point in education, one with far reaching implications, that is changing and continue to change everything about learning, work and human purpose." (Page xxxiii)[5]

4. AI has captured significant popular attention. For example, at the World Government Summit in Dubai in 2015, Klaus Schwab, the executive chairman of the *World Economic Forum*, announced that "you will no longer be using an app to call a human Uber driver (to say nothing of driving your own car), but instead, you would be hiring a driverless vehicle to "take you to the airport."[6]

In this chapter, I will set forth AI as another stage in the evolution of automation. I have separated AI from other, earlier stages of automation

---

[2] https://www.intelligentcio.com/north-america/2024/08/08/usa-leading-the-charge-on-ai-investment/#:~:text=The%20US%20invests%20the%20most,less%20than%20the%20United%20States.

[3] https://www.euronews.com/next/2025/02/11/eu-to-mobilise-200-billion-for-ai-investment.

[4] https://www.forbes.com/sites/jilliandonfro/2019/09/17/ai-50-americas-most-promising-artificial-intelligence-companies/.

[5] Khan (2024).

[6] https://forbiddenknowledgetv.net/klaus-schwab-los-angeles-to-be-private-car-driven-free-by-2030/.

for two reasons. First, AI continues to evolve, and hence our understanding of AI is rudimentary, i.e., without complete evidence and hence filled with judgments often biased but made with incomplete information. Second, recent advances in AI have given rise to fears regarding human control of societies, fears that may influence the evolution and implementation of AI in organizations.

In successive sections, I will touch upon the concept of AI, its evolution, and its anticipated impact on work and employment. Finally, I will highlight the key factors driving the fears associated with AI, fears that are different from their direct impact on work.

What is Artificial Intelligence?

Although AI may refer to computer systems that can perform complex tasks normally done by human reasoning, decision making, or creativity, there is *no* single, simple definition of AI because AI tools are capable of a wide range of tasks and outputs. For example, according to Google, "Artificial intelligence is a field of science concerned with building computers and machines that can *reason, learn, and act in such a way that would normally require human intelligence* or that involves data whose scale exceeds what humans can analyze."[7] A more detailed version formulated by, NASA defines AI as:

- Any artificial system that performs tasks under varying and unpredictable circumstances without significant human oversight, or that can learn from experience and improve performance when exposed to data sets.
- An artificial system developed in computer software, physical hardware, or other context that solves tasks requiring human-like perception, cognition, planning, learning, communication, or physical action.
- An artificial system that is designed to think or act like a human, including cognitive architecture and neural networks.[8]
- A set of techniques, including machine learning, that is designed to approximate a cognitive task.

---

[7] https://cloud.google.com/learn/what-is-artificial-intelligence.

[8] https://www.nasa.gov/what-is-artificial-intelligence/.

- An artificial system that is designed to act rationally, including an intelligent software agent or embodied robot that achieves goals using perception, planning, reasoning, learning, communicating, decision-making, and acting.

NASA has followed the (US) National Defense Authorization Act of 2019 (Summarized in Box 1).

Underneath this complexity lie six major technical developments: Machine Learning (ML), Deep Learning, Decision Support, Large Language Models (LLM), neural networks, and Robotic Process Automation (RPA).

Machine learning uses data and algorithms to train computers to make classifications, generate predictions, or uncover similarities or trends across large datasets.

Deep learning is a subset of machine learning that involves neural networks with many layers. It distinguishes itself from other forms of neural networks primarily through its capability to learn features automatically from data.

Decision support requires tools to consider imperfect or unknown situations. This method of AI considers multiple outcomes and probabilities to inform decisions.

Large language models enable machines to understand language and generate human-like text with unprecedented accuracy and have opened new avenues for applications such as chatbots and virtual assistants (Gefen *et al.*, 2024).[9]

Neural networks, a method to train computers to process data in a way that's inspired by the human brain by using a layered, interconnected neuron-inspired structure.

---

[9]AI chatbots are trained on large amounts of data and use ML to intelligently generate a wide range of non-scripted, conversational responses to human text and voice input. Virtual agents are AI bots that can be specifically trained to interact with customers in call centers or contact centers.

Box 1 . 2025 National Defense Authorization Act.*

The Act (NDAA) includes several provisions to use artificial intelligence (AI) to improve defense operations. The NDAA aims to use AI in cybersecurity, biotechnology, and other areas, and establishes guidelines to reduce the risk of adversaries using AI against the United States. [1, 2, 3] Key provisions include [1]:

- *Research and development*: Prioritize research on AI and quantum computing [1].
- *Pilot programs*: Establish pilot programs to use AI in manufacturing, contract administration, and biotechnology [2, 4].
- *Working groups*: Establish a working group to develop AI initiatives with allies and partners [4, 5, 6].
- *AI-related programs*: Establish a center of excellence to develop AI-enabled weapon systems [2].
- *AI workforce*: Integrate and train the Department of Defense (DoD) workforce in AI [2].
- *AI risk mitigation*: Establish guidelines to reduce the risk of adversaries using AI against the United States [1].
- *Policy statement*: Establish a Statement of Policy regarding the use of AI in nuclear weaponry systems [5].

The NDAA was passed by Congress in December 2024 [3].

[1] https://www.klgates.com/Key-Provisions-on-Artificial-Intelligence-in-Fiscal-Year-2025-NDAA-1-2-2025.
[2] https://perkinscoie.com/insights/update/fy-2025-national-defense-authorization-act-whats-new-defense-contractors.
[3] https://natlawreview.com/article/congress-passes-defense-bill-ai-provisions-ai-washington-report.
[4] https://www.mlstrategies.com/insights-center/viewpoints/54031/2024-12-19-congress-passes-defense-bill-ai-provisions-ai.
[5] https://www.nextgov.com/emerging-tech/2024/12/fy2025-ndaa-angles-enhance-dods-ai-and-quantum-sciences-capabilities/401545/.
[6] https://www.akingump.com/en/insights/alerts/senate-leaders-file-ndaa-package-with-ai-provisions-setting-the-stage-for-lame-duck-negotiations.

*Box 1 was produced using generative AI.

Robotic process automation, or bots, which automate routine and repetitive tasks (Gefen *et al.*, 2024).

Both technology convergence and the development of ancillary technologies have enabled the development of AI applications in organizations. I will touch upon its evolution, which continues to date, as this monograph goes to the press.

AI Evolution

The origin of AI dates back to work on problem solving by Newell and Simon in Carnegie and Minsky and McCarthy at MIT (Hunt, 2014),[10] both during the 1960s. These pioneers of AI were focused on fundamental questions. For example, Newell and Simon were interested in problem solving and also wanted to create (geometric) theorem-solving machines. It is only in recent years that AI tools have been adopted in organizations. Unlike the general questions that interested its pioneers, AI implementation in organizations has focused on its applications. Partly as a result, AI applications have evolved quickly.

Techno optimists like Khan and Schwab, who recognize the technical potential of AI (and associated technologies), are not primarily focused on work, but instead on the pathways by which technological development can enrich human life in general. They focus on the functionality of AI and its furtherment. The functionality hinges on three critical capabilities of AI:

(1) It can adjust to *new* inputs;
(2) it can *learn* from experience; and
(3) it can perform *human-like* tasks. Today's generation of AI technologies exploits AI's functionalities, in the process making the benefits of AI clear to a growing number of individuals. As illustrated by McKinsey[11]:

---

[10] Hunt (2014).

[11] McKinsey, compiled from articles by McKinsey. https://www.mckinsey.com/capabilities/quantumblack/our-insights.

- AI adds intelligence to existing products, much like Siri was added as a feature to Apple phones. Technology confluence is at work; automation, conversational platforms, bots, and smart machines can be combined with large amounts of data to improve many technologies.
- AI adapts through progressive learning algorithms to let the data do the programming. The recent statement by Satya Nadella, the CEO of Microsoft, that "Saas is dead,"[12] is illustrative of the growing role of AI in shaping software delivery and consumption.
- AI analyzes more and deeper data using neural networks. They have many hidden layers, and this is essential to activities like fraud detection.
- AI achieves incredible accuracy and is seamlessly incorporated into products used daily by humans, such as Alexa and Google.

The speed with which technology confluence is progressing, combining technologies within AI and outside for applications, has been impressive (Acemoglu and Restrepo, 2020).[13] Just as this monograph is being written, the concepts of *digital workers* and *avatars* have already come into the lexicon.

- Whereas a bot can be programmed to execute tasks, a digital worker can do much more. "Digital workers understand human interaction. They are configured to respond to questions and act on a human's behalf" (Gefen *et al.*, 2025).
- An AI avatar is a computer-generated image of a person that uses AI (using machine learning, facial recognition, and 3D modeling) to mimic human characteristics — a person's appearance, expressions, gestures, and even their voice. In the workplace, they are increasingly used to streamline production and connect with diverse audiences; on websites, AI avatars can also be used for customer support, training, or sales.

---

[12] https://procureinsights.com/2025/01/16/why-did-satya-nadella-say-that-saas-is-dead-and-what-does-it-mean-for-erp-platforms/#:~:text=Conclusion,value%2C%20efficiency%2C%20and%20adaptability.&text=Everything%20outlined%20above%20seems%20reasonable,than%20r.

[13] Acemoglu and Restrepo (2020). Autor *et al.* (2003).

Effects on Employment

Because AI as a technology or tool is still evolving and organizations are experimenting with ways to incorporate AI in their operations, it would be premature to posit definitive conclusions about the impact of AI on employment No doubt, it will take some time before we can clearly create and understand the empirical evidence of AI" s influence on employment, It is worth repeating: AI is *a story in progress*. Therefore, it is prudent to keep in mind the cautionary note provided by MIT researchers:

> AI is really different; it may substitute some high-skill expertise but may complement decision-making tasks. I think we're in an era where we have this new tool, and we don't know what's good for. New technologies have strengths and weaknesses, and it takes a while to figure them out. GPS was invented for military purposes, and it took decades for it to be in smartphones (Autor *et al.*, 2003).[14]

The scholarship of employment effects of AI, even those with limited evidence, can be broadly summarized into three: (1) jobs that are likely to be destroyed; (2) jobs that are likely to be created; and (3) the sectors most affected.

Job replacement: There has been growing recognition that AI can be deployed in multiple task domains and can therefore be regarded as a general-purpose technology (Bresnahan and Trajtenberg, 1995). General-purpose technologies become pervasive, improve over time, and generate complementary innovation. Job replacement theorists typically view AI as an instance of capital replacing labor. Because AI can perform tasks usually requiring specific human skills related to visual perception, speech, sentiment recognition, and decision-making, compared to previous waves of automation, "AI is replacing mental tasks rather than physical ones" (Ernst *et al.*, 2019). This replacement is taking place in performing prediction tasks, i.e., tasks based on using existing data to fill in missing information, decision tasks, i.e., tasks based on an ability to take action based on a decision, and judgment to evaluate the payoffs associated with different outcomes.

[14] Acemoglu and Restrepo (2020).

Job creation: Scholars who have viewed AI as a creator of job opportunities, have claimed that AI should be viewed as a platform, which can be used not only to automate tasks, but also to restructure production process in a way that creates many new high productivity tasks in such fields as education, health care, and augmented reality (Acemoglu and Restrepo, 2019; Mondolo, 2020).[15] Although they concede that labor enabling technologies may create human stunting (injury, reduced physical and mental health, reduction of autonomy, privacy, and human dignity), they also create an opportunity for human augmentation (to enhance excellence, experience a sense of community, and contribute to society. (Furendal and Jebari, 2023).[16]

Sectors: The current interest in AI, unlike in robotics or automation, stems from the fact that AI can provide human-like interactions. It is expected that significant facets of service industries (e.g., education, banking, health care, and accounting) can be automated with AI. Although AI may not obliterate many of these jobs, it is now recognized that AI can provide significant decision support for many of these tasks. For example, its role in research, a task generally regarded as creative and thus requiring human involvement, is well illustrated by the recent publicized research, which used ChatGPT to identify patterns in the voice data of elephants.[17]

In the absence of valid and reliable data, discussions of AI's influence are filled with judgments and opinions, hopes and fears. At the risk of simplification, these opinions can be categorized into three: techno optimists, managerialists, and Luddites. Techno optimists like Khan and Schwab (quoted earlier in the chapter) see the possibilities opened by AI; managerialists are most closely aligned with the optimists and see

[15] Mondolo (2022).

[16] Furendal and Jebari (2023).

[17] The study, titled "African savannah elephants call one another by 'name'," was published on 10 June 2024 in the journal *Nature Ecology & Evolution*. The authors, comprising researchers from the US, Kenya, and Norway, said, "Using a combination of machine learning and playback experiments in the field, we find that African savannah elephants address members of their family with individually specific, name-like calls. These 'names' are probably not imitative of the receiver's calls, which is similar to human naming but unlike known phenomena in other animals."

development of AI in terms of productivity gains,[18] whereas the Luddites predictably are worried about the negative effects on employment.

AI will certainly accelerate the automation of routine activities. Robo vacuums, Google Assistant, and Alexa have all now entered the market with others such as self-driven cars to follow. But what of judgment and decision-related activities in managerial tasks? This remains the major unanswered question: How do AI and AI-linked applications affect the managerial level? It is now becoming clear that a lot of routine activities built into managerial work can be automated with the help of AI. Indeed, if Gefen and his colleagues are to be believed, it is easy to visualize managers having their own digital *assistants* to help them with their routine tasks. Whether AI can do non-routine tasks is still being debated, and I will pick that theme up in the next chapter. Although we do not have definitive answers, in the next chapter, I will employ an organizational framework put forth by Talcott Parsons to think about this issue.

Techno-optimists cheer on, but their concern is not merely the managers but the humans in general — making their lives simpler and perhaps more convenient. The fears generated by AI, however, span more issues than employment, and these fears have the potential to influence the development of AI. I will briefly touch upon these fears.

AI and Locus of Control

During the 1960s, Frank Hebert,[19] the famous science fiction writer, conceived of *Omnius*, a collection of powerful artificially intelligent entities, to foreshadow the events in his now famous *Dune* trilogy. Omnius represented a stage in the evolution of technology when humanity had relinquished its freedom and right to live to AI or Thinking Machines, as they were called in the saga. AI took more and more control of human lives, until, in the end, they became not so much as autonomous but independent of human control. Finally, they ruled the Empire somewhat tyrannically.

As many prior science fiction stories have done before, *Dune* portrayed how the rapid development of computers raised the specter of the

---

[18] For example, consulting firms like McKinsey have been proclaiming the benefits of SI. See, for example, https://www.mckinsey.com/capabilities/mckinsey-digital/our-insights/the-economic-potential-of-generative-ai-the-next-productivity-frontier.

[19] Frank Herbert was an American science-fiction writer noted as the author of the best-selling Dune series of futuristic novels, a group of highly complex works.

loss of human control, not merely of the workplace but of lives in general. Recent concerns about AI are eerily reminiscent of some of these fears, which may have a profound influence on the evolution of AI technology. These fears have been raised by cognitive psychologists such as Steven Pinker, business leaders like Eric Schmidt, and political philosophers like Henry Kissinger. At the time of this writing, I can identify three clusters of related factors (Kissinger *et al.*, 2024):

1. *Fear of outpacing human capabilities*: Much like in the case of Omnius, many intellectuals are concerned that AI tools have already started outpacing human capabilities.
2. *Biological engineering efforts for tighter human fusion with machines*: Marked by the US Military as of utmost importance, human-computer interfaces allow for a direct link between the brain and computers.
3. *Altering the genetic code*: Pushed by technological development, society chooses to create a hereditary genetic line of people specifically designed to work with AI tools, or in other words, a race that is seen as superior.

At the base of all these fears is the fear of impending loss of control by human beings of their own destiny. Of course, many prescriptions are put forth. For one, Steven Pinker urges more careful attention to the design of AI tools, suggesting that engineers who design AI tools look beyond the solution to the technical problem to larger societal concerns. Kissinger and his co-authors want engineers to make machines more human, rather than make humans more like machines. Solutions notwithstanding, the fears have raised the possibility that technological evolution in the AI domain is likely to be controlled by social concerns. The position is voiced by Kissinger *et al.* (2024):

> We ... cannot rely solely on the supposition that machines will tame themselves...Training AI to understand us and then sitting back and hoping that it respects us is not a strategy that seems either safe or likely to succeed.

Kissinger *et al.* (2024) have — rightfully in my opinion — questioned the assumptions that are fueling the current development of AI. Their concerns are societal and thus more encompassing than the concerns with work addressed in this book. I am focused narrowly on uncovering a major assumption that has underpinned most discussions about the influence of automation in general, and especially AI, on employment. In the next chapter, I will argue that AI may render our conception of work — a conception that was incubated during the industrial age — obsolete.

References

Acemoglu, D. and Restrepo, P. (2020). The wrong kind of AI? Artificial intelligence and the future of labour demand. *Cambridge Journal of Regions, Economy and Society*, 13(1), 25–35.

Autor, D. H., Levy, F., and Murnane, R. J. (2003). The skill content of recent technological change: An empirical exploration. *The Quarterly journal of economics*, 118(4), 1279–1333.

Bresnahan, T. F. and Trajtenberg, M. (1995). General purpose technologies 'Engines of growth'? *Journal of Econometrics*, 65(1), 83–108.

Ernst, E., Merola, R., and Samaan, D. (2019). Economics of artificial intelligence: Implications for the future of work. *IZA Journal of Labor Policy*, 9(1), 1–35.

Furendal, M. and Jebari, K. (2023). The future of work: Augmentation or stunting? *Philosophy & Technology*, 36(2), 36.

Hunt, E. B. (2014). *Artificial Intelligence*. Academic Press.

Khan, S. (2024). *Brave New Words: How AI Will Revolutionize Education (and Why That's a Good Thing)*. Penguin.

Kissinger, H. A., Schmidt, E., and Mundie, C. (2024). *Genesis: Artificial Intelligence, Hope, and the Human Spirit*. Little, Brown.

Mondolo, J. (2022). The composite link between technological change and employment: A survey of the literature. *Journal of Economic Surveys*, 36(4), 1027–1068.

Chapter 7

Workless Society

Abstract

I make the argument that in most recent academic analyses, we have taken for granted the assumption that work is ubiquitous and necessary, overlooking the possibility that work may not be necessary. I recapitulate the earlier chapters by noting that we have narrowed the meaning of work to a set of activities that human beings as employees do in industrial settings. Technological change obviates the need for several activities that constitute "work." Automation has obviated the need for repetitive tasks or what Talcott Parsons characterized as the technical level of an organization. Technical advances of the last decade, broadly termed digitalization, are making it possible to automate managerial work. The debates about AI are significantly focused on its implications for employment, overlooking the possibility that work as currently conceived may not be necessary.

Work Revisited

What is work? Why should human beings work? As I have demonstrated in the previous chapters, these are significant questions that have attracted scholarly attention over the last several decades. Indeed, our conception of work has evolved over the years in three crucial ways:

1. Instead of being an abstraction, work is indeed a concrete *bundle of activities* influenced by human decisions, operating context, and technological change. In the previous chapters, I have shown how

(1) management theorists provided a set of tools and frameworks to design work in an organization; (2) work-related activities can be influenced by context, particularly government intervention; and (3) technological change can alter work activities, for example, automation has obviated the need for humans doing repetitive work.

2. As societies settled into agriculture, evolving away from being hunter-gatherer societies, activity structures in living units got somewhat specialized, with men undertaking outward activities and women taking care of family matters. Further, as industrial societies came into existence, nuclear families emerged and intensified the specialization of activities, especially between man and woman. *Work as we know it* came into existence. Human beings began working in factories and organizations outside of their homes, exchanging labor for remuneration. The transactional conception of work was born, and it got a foothold in organizations in which human beings toiled.
3. Reflecting the ethos of the Gilded Age, Thorstein Veblen distinguished leisure from work. In the process, he provided a conceptual basis for the stratification of societies: those who engage in work and those who could afford to pursue leisure, whom he called the leisure class. He underscored the transactional dimension of work: Employees gave their time and effort in exchange for monetary remuneration, not necessarily because they undertook work activities for intrinsic rewards. Thus, the leisure class enjoyed a higher status in societies because they were not motivated by the remuneration from work activities.

Over the course of the last half of 20th century, when management theorists grappled with the question of what motivates human beings, they were inspired by the writings of Abraham Maslow.[1] Maslow set forth a

---

[1] Abraham Harold Maslow was an American psychologist and philosopher who established humanistic psychology alongside Carl Rogers. He is best known for the theory of the hierarchy of needs, a theory that explains the spectrum of human needs, from basic physiological needs like food and shelter to complex social needs like respect. Maslow believed that people have an innate urge for self-actualization, but that this desire only surfaces after more basic needs are met. See https://www.google.com/search?gs_ssp=eJzj4tTP1TcwLIpPKzdg9OJLTCpKzEjMVchNLM7JLwcAc2sI9g&q=abraham+maslow&rlz=1C1GCEV_enUS991US992&oq=Abrah&gs_lcrp=EgZjaHJvbWUqDwgCEC4YQxixAxiABBiKBT-ISCAAQABhDGOMCGLEDGIAEGIoFMg8IARAuGEMYsQMYgAQYigUyDwgCEC4YQxixAxiABBiKBTINCAMQLhjUAhixAxiABDIGCAQQRRg5MgoIBR

five-tier model of human needs arranged in a hierarchy, the five tiers being physiological, safety, love/belonging, esteem, and self-actualization. Although Maslow did not consider the order of tiers as completely fixed, he believed that lower-level basic needs like food, water, and safety must be met first before higher needs can be fulfilled. There has been a healthy discussion among management theories as to the role of the workplace: whether it should aspire to provide employees with settings for self-actualization. Some enlightened thinkers like Chris Argyris[2] advocated that option, whereas others pointed out that self-actualization need not be confined to organizational settings. Both groups understood that in the industrial era, work had a *transactional* quality: Bluntly stated, employees go to work to put food on their family's table, whether they self-actualized or not.

This *necessity* of work to meet the lower-level needs of employees in modern industrial societies has led to an intellectual byproduct: We have begun to take work for granted on the assumption that the existence of work needs no explanation. As we have seen in the previous chapters, roboticization has decimated blue-collar work, and the attendant technical layer of Parson's organization model (To be discussed in the next section), and digitization, especially AI, has begun to erode the need for *humans* in managerial work. However, the rapidly arising possibilities from automation are often discussed *within* the assumption that work is inevitable. Thus, the opportunity to *imagine* a society without work or composed of only the "leisure class," to use Thorstein Veblen's terms, is not addressed in much of our writing. I examine this in the context of the crucial issues that have received attention in the context of Artificial Intelligence (AI), or more broadly, digitalization.

This chapter is organized into three sections. First, I will utilize Talcott Parsons's model of organization to frame the impact of automation, both roboticization and AI, or more inclusively, digitalization. Second, I will summarize the arguments for the two different aspects of AI — employment

AuGLEDGIAEMgwIBhAuGEMYgAQYigUyEAgHEC4YrwEYxwEYgAQYjgUyDQgIEC4YgwEYsQMYgAQyBwgJEAAYjwLSAQg2ODc0ajBqN6gCALACAA&sourceid=chrome&ie=UTF-8.

[2]Chris Argyris was an American business theorist and professor at Yale School of Management and Harvard Business School. Argyris, like Richard Beckhard, Edgar Schein, and Warren Bennis, is known as a co-founder of organization development, and known for seminal work on learning organizations.

and control. Finally, I highlight the taken-for-granted assumption in these discussions, that work is ubiquitous.

Talcott Parsons's Organizational Model: AI's Impact on Organizations

Talcott Parsons was an influential American sociologist who brought Max Weber's work to America, built a multidisciplinary social sciences approach at Harvard, and developed a highly integrated and complex theory of social action (Heckscher, 2015). Parsons was a systematizer, passionate about grasping everything within a single coherent theoretical framework: the theory of the social system. He provided theoretical inspiration to many later sociologists, such as J. D. Thompson,[3] whose work laid the foundations of modern organization theory.

Parsons argued that organizations operate at three levels of responsibility: technical, managerial, and institutional.

1. The *technical* core is responsible for producing the product or service output of organizations, i.e., the conversion of raw materials into products and services. For example, in school districts, teachers teaching students are direct workers and constitute the technical core, tending to influence student educational development (Daft and Becker, 1980).
2. The *managerial level* is that part of the organization responsible for designing and controlling the production system, for procuring inputs and disposing of outputs, and for securing and allocating personnel to units and functions. The managerial level mediates between

---

[3]James Thompson was an American sociologist. His Wikipedia entry notes the following:

> *Organizations in Action* was published in 1967. The book is still today a classic multidisciplinary study of the behavior of complex organizations as entities. …Thompson saw technology as a dimension in understanding the actions of complex organization. Thompson recognized the benefit for managers of using a typology of technology that could be general enough to deal with a different range of technologies found in complex organizations.

an organization and its external environment. Managers are also responsible for administering internal affairs, coordinating activities, and making decisions that align with the organization's goals. Examples of managerial roles include department heads, supervisors, and team leaders.

3. Finally, the *institutional level* relates the organization to its wider environment (such as government agencies, regulatory bodies, and community organizations), determines its domain, establishes its boundaries, and secures its legitimacy. Thus, relationships with organizations and other elements in the external environment represent activity at the institutional level of responsibility. Examples of institutional roles include chief executive officers and board members.

In Figure 1, we have summarized the framework presented by Parsons.

Within this framework, human beings organize work-related activities in a hierarchy, with repetitive work at the lowest level, computational and judgmental at the middle level, and mission-related activities at the institutional level. Given the nature of Talcott Parsons's hierarchy, the humans at the technical level are more numerous than at the middle or top levels of

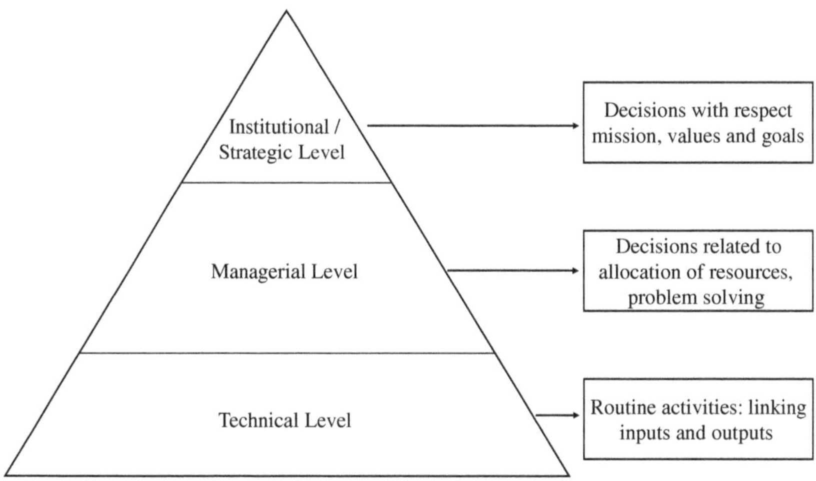

Fig. 1. Talcott Parsons's model.

organization. It is generally accepted that the technical level consists mostly of repetitive activities, e.g., the job of blue-collar workers in relation to their assembly line jobs. The managerial level is more complex: While there are numerous routine activities (e.g., data entry), these jobs also ostensibly include judgment and decision-making, activities that include non-routine components. Non-routine components are typically believed to be non-repetitive. Institutional-level tasks are generally considered to be human activities as they address the realm of human values.

In the previous two chapters, I touched upon three successive waves of automation: roboticization, digitalization, and AI. Parsons also provides a convenient, albeit incomplete, framework to examine some of the organizational impact of automation.

Roboticization. It is clear that roboticization enables the automation of repetitive activities, substituting technology for human labor. Stated differently, in Parsons's framework, robots make it possible to automate the technical level of organization, reducing, if not obliterating, the need for any humans in routine task activities. As we have shown in Fig. 2 on page 75, the modern "shop floor" is almost devoid of human labor. Scholarly evidence also points to the fact that roboticization has depleted the ranks of the blue-collar workforce.

The challenge is to stipulate the impact on organizations of digitalization, especially AI.

Digitalization. Within Talcott Parsons's framework, we can without much difficulty accept the conclusion that digitization will accelerate the automation of repetitive tasks (the technical level). Thus, the adoption of ICT has decimated the ranks of data entry jobs. It has also enabled the automation of blue-collar jobs by allowing some logical operations to be taken over by computers. Thus, the early stages of digitalization have primarily affected the technical level of the organizational hierarchy.

Historical precedents would suggest that while some sectors of employment will be adversely affected by digitization, the need for higher-level skills in augmenting technologies may, however, generate employment. Recall that augmenting technologies enable a new technology to extend human capabilities in physical performance, cognitive function, and sensory perception through integration with machines, devices or external systems. For example, the technology confluence between digitization and virtual reality has enabled doctors to monitor and/ or diagnose diseases based on various tests. Augmenting technologies do not map conveniently onto Parsons's framework. They demand higher skill levels and *possibly* could be automated, but whether they can *really* be automated is at the moment an open question.

So, the uncertainty is with respect to the *managerial level*. Managerial tasks are assumed to be non-routine because they involve judgment and decision-making. The arrival of AI has pried open our beliefs about the extent to which managerial jobs can be automated.

Artificial Intelligence (AI) and Parsons's Model

As noted previously in digitalization, AI will undoubtedly hasten the automation of the activities at the technical level and some layers of the managerial level in Parsons's organizational model. In addition, the currently held assumption about non-routine managerial activities is vulnerable to the emerging characteristics of AI (Kissinger *et al.*, 2024).

A number of characteristics set AI apart from traditional ICTs:

1. AI is capable of *synthesizing* several bits of diverse information to arrive at a *conclusion* — in response to a query in Chat GPT — unlike conventional search engines such as Google. AI can do it quite fast; AI is superior in its speed capabilities to humans.
2. AI has the capability of *learning* from new bits of information, and unlike a rules (preprogrammed) based order, AI learns from its experience.
3. AI, because it is emotion *free*, can lead to conclusions without fear and bias, unlike human beings, thus stripping judgment from human fallacies.
4. AI performance has shown that it can *reach conclusions* that humans have not been able to: witness its performance in chess relative to humans.
5. Specific to managerial tasks, AI is rapidly developing its capability in *planning*. Although the current models allow forecasting of the probable consequences, only within limited and highly abstract frames, "the arrival of a 'perfect planner' may occur sooner than we expect" (Kissinger *et al.*, 2024, p. 64).

These and other characteristics of AI call into question the assumption that AI does not have problem-solving abilities or, in other words, cannot perform non-routine tasks. Many of the jobs and the activities that are associated with AI, that we have assumed to be impervious to obsolescence because of technological development, may not really be so. Here is a prediction from Bill Gates[4]:

> ... The era we've come to is sort of the vision that computing was expensive, and it basically became free. The era that we're just starting is that intelligence is rare, you know, a great doctor, a great teacher. And with AI, over the next decade, that will become free. Commonplace, you know? Great medical advice, great tutoring.

I have noted earlier that AI is a story in *progress*. Currently, AI systems can conduct face recognition, speech to text conversion, and language translation; navigate roads well enough for autonomous driving; compose texts with great detail; and even compose music. This is only for now. To get a glimpse of where it is headed, let me quote Suleyman (Suleyman, 2023, p. 29),[5] founder of DeepMind[6]:

> Even in more challenging domains, ones thought to be uniquely suited to human capabilities like long-term planning, imagination and simulation of complex ideas, progress leaps forward.
>
> AI has been climbing the ladder of cognitive abilities for decades, and it looks set to reach human level performance across a wide range of tasks within the next three years. This is a big claim, but if I am even close to right, the implications are truly profound.

The characteristics of AI and the present trajectory of its development suggest that AI may simply automate the managerial layer of the Parsons model. If both technical and managerial layers are automated in ways that are superior in performance to those by human beings, only the institutional layer remains in the control of humans, but more pertinent to the theme of this manuscript, only institutional tasks need to be performed by

---

[4] Gates, https://people.com/bill-gates-ai-will-replace-doctors-teachers-in-next-10-years-11705615.

[5] Mustafa Suleyman is currently the CEO of *Microsoft AI*, and the co-founder and former head of applied AI at DeepMind, an AI company acquired by Google. After leaving DeepMind, he co-founded *Inflection AI*, a machine learning and generative AI company.

[6] Suleyman (2023). chrome-extension://efaidnbmnnnibpcajpcglclefindmkaj/https://www.bls.gov/news.release/pdf/empsit.pdf.

humans. The next stage in the development of AI, Artificial General Intelligence (AGI), is expected to bestow it with the ability to choose its own goals. These developments are knocking on the doors of what we have to date assumed to be the domain of unquestionably human activities.

This takes me to the central theme of this work: *We may need to question the assumption that humans need to work.* We cannot escape the unavoidable conjecture of a workless society, however far-fetched that may appear to us today.

The Assumption of Work as Ubiquitous

Work as ubiquitous

We have seen in our earlier chapters that work, *as we know it*, originated in the industrial age. Today, the concept of work is taken for granted and is widely shared among individuals. Few dispute the assumption that humans need to engage in work. Associated with this assumption is the corollary notion of an organization, where work is being carried out.

How is this possible? In March 2025, the US Bureau of Labor Statistics reported that the total non-farm payroll employment rose by 228,000, and the unemployment rate changed little at 4.2%, one of the lowest in recent US history.[7] Further, nearly 5% of the population, or over 8 million people, have multiple jobs, the highest since the Great Recession of 2009. Doesn't the US economy give the lie to the idea of a workless society? But as I have demonstrated, automation over its history has rendered the technical level of an organization, with its three-tier structure of activities (as modeled by Parsons), unnecessary, and the impending development in AI has the potential to make the managerial level obsolete as well. Thus, it is not the possibility of a workless society but the actuality of it that is in question.

And here, I will posit that our lack of questioning of the need for work is provoked by the tacit but influential assumption that work is ubiquitous and does not need an explanation. For example, our discussions about technological development in AI have vacillated between managerialist and Luddite polarities. Managerialist perspectives typically focus on

---

[7]US Bureau of Labor Statistics. Employment Situation, News release, April 4, 2025.

talent scarcity, development of tools for enhancing productivity, and identifying sectors and areas where AI can now be deployed. Luddite perspectives focus on the other end of the spectrum, raising concerns about employment and fear of widespread layoffs among middle management ranks. These are important issues, no doubt, but they are all rooted in the tacit assumption that the need for work needs no explanation.

This is a failure of imagination. Our analyses seem to be exercises in "single-loop learning" (Argyris), which do not address some of the fundamental assumptions that maintain our vision of the current social order. If we cannot imagine it, it cannot inform or influence our discussions, the options we consider, and the policy levers we may employ. That is a missed opportunity.

A "workless" society may share some of the characteristics of Veblen's leisure class. But there is a major difference. Veblen's leisure class created social stratification: There was a leisure class of wealthy individuals and a working class of middle- or lower-class individuals. But a "workless" society is characterized by *mass* leisure. Unlike the Gilded Age, Veblen reflected that — with relatively low levels of technological development — a workless society is anchored in a technological regime that has obliterated the need for manual activity to satisfy basic human needs.

A workless society is currently an assumption that depends on technological progress. Those who are involved in technological development are often carried away by lofty ideals. As extolled by Ferguson in his commentary on Kissinger *et al.* (2024), AI could be harnessed for the following:

> To generate a new baseline of human wealth and well-being.....[that] would at least ease if not eliminate the strains of labor, class, and conflict that have torn humanity apart... The adoption of AI might even lead to profound equalization, across race, gender, nationality, place of birth and family background.[8,9]

However, an assumption of a workless society is not likely to be driven by technology alone; technologists may not even be the major

---

[8] Ferguson, in Kissinger *et al.* (2024), p. xix.

[9] The quote is by a historian in a book where two other authors are in the forefront of pushing technology.

players in societal architecture. Thus, the euphoria of a potentially workless society needs to be weighed against the challenges. Indeed, a society based on mass leisure has to grapple with certain challenges. Leisure has its discontents. We will pick this theme up in the next chapter.

References

Daft, R. and Becker, S. W. (1980). Managerial, institutional, and technical influences on administration: A longitudinal analysis. *Social Forces*, 59(2), 392–413. https://doi.org/10.1093/sf/59.2.392.

Heckscher, C. (2015). From bureaucracy to networks. In *The SAGE Handbook of the Sociology of Work and Employment*, UK: Sage Publications, pp. 245–258.

Kissinger, H. A., Schmidt, E., and Mundie, C. (2024). *Genesis: Artificial Intelligence, Hope, and the Human Spirit*. New York: Little, Brown.

Suleyman, M. (2023). *The Coming Wave: Technology, Power, and the Twenty-First Century's Greatest Dilemma*. New York: Crown.

Chapter 8

Workless Society: Challenges

Abstract

It is one thing to conceive of a workless society, another to visualize how to get there, or, for that matter, how to live in that society. In this chapter, I address the scarcity mindset and the need for control as two fundamental barriers to the acceptance of the assumption. Over our evolutionary history, humans have grown up to recognize the world as resource-scarce, and control is built into the working of modern-day organizations, where most work is carried out. In addition, a workless society where leisure or, more correctly, non-work is prevalent, is likely to face significant challenges arising from the release of time from work. In order, I will touch upon both the barriers to and challenges of a workless society.

As I documented in the prior chapter, the new wave of technological change ushered in by AI has brought the specter of fully automated organizations, where the manual input required is minimal and much of what we have considered work to date is done by robots in digital factories that leverage the potential of AI. Thus, we are at the doorstep of a *workless* society, or to use Veblen's words, a society in which the modal population is engaged in leisure activities.

Already there are *weak* signals of the emergence of a new societal landscape. Although not exhaustive, let me cite three of these signals. First, a recent issue of The *Economist* (2025) reported that in the world's richer economies, "inheritocracy" (their term) or inheriting "is becoming nearly as important as working."

> People in advanced economies stand to inherit around $6trn this year — about 10% GDP, up from around 5% on average in a selection of rich countries during the middle of the 20th century. … Whether a young person can afford to buy a house and live in relative comfort is determined by the inherited wealth nearly as much as it is by their own success at work. These "trust fund babies" existed even before the Gilded Age (the time of Veblen's writing), but sheer number of these folks today is a new phenomenon.

Second, there is reason to believe that basic needs of humans — food, shelter, and clothing — *are* increasingly met, for large swaths of population, partly because of the productivity gains in the last century. Take, for example, the case of food, which is not only a basic necessity for survival but also a driving force behind a nation's economic prosperity. In 2020, Bloomberg reported that the global food production stood at approximately 4 billion metric tons annually. This is expected to rise along with per capita food consumption. Over the decades, since 1961, there has been a consistent global uptrend in the per capita calorie supply, reflecting changes and advancements in food production, distribution, and consumption patterns worldwide.[1] Sure enough, there have been and continue to be wide disparities among nations, partly due to distribution inefficiencies. Moreover, Forbes estimated that global food waste is well on the way to becoming a billion-ton problem, and the United Nations Environment Programme's 2021 Food Waste Index has found that an estimated 931 million tons of food end up in the trash every year.[2] Most of that figure falls under the category of household waste, while the food service and retail sectors also waste food considerably.

Finally, a *small* group of scholars has begun to argue that humanity has reached a stage where the most basic needs of humans are fulfilled without much effort. Here is Steven Pinker,[3] author and professor of cognitive science at Harvard University:

> In the 19th century, Westerners worked more than 60 hours per week. Today, they work fewer than 40. Thanks to the universal penetration of

---

[1] https://ourworldindata.org/food-supply.

[2] file:///C:/Users/vkn22/Downloads/FoodWaste.pdf.

[3] Steven Pinker is a cognitive psychologist and linguist known for his books on language, mind, and human progress. His popular works, such as *The Language Instinct* and *Enlightenment Now*, present optimistic, data-driven views on human development and rationality.

> running water and electricity in the developed world and the widespread adoption of washing machines, vacuum cleaners, refrigerators, dishwashers, stoves and microwaves, the amount of our lives that we forfeit to housework has fallen from 60 hours a week to fewer than 15 hours a week.[4]

Consistent with the aims of this monograph, I would like to emphasize that most of the "consumer durables" Pinker mentions have *automated away the work activities* that, at least in the developed economies, had been a regular part of individuals' lives.

However, the journey toward a workless society is fraught with three obstacles, all of human making: the challenges inherent in a leisureful society, the scarcity mindset, and human desire for power and control. We start with the natural consequences, which present enormous human challenges, because a workless society will have to contend with the natural consequences of mass leisure.

Leisure and its Discontents

I would advance the not-so-appreciated idea that non-work has its discontents. If one reads Veblen and the sociology that he portrays, the leisure class, with its presumed superiority, is an ineluctable group to belong to. Because members of this class do not have to work, the leisure class is deemed superior. We are often carried away by its mystique, and many of us envy its members. But what would a workless society look like, other than there is no compulsion to go to work?

In the following, I would enumerate two sets of major challenges presented by a workless society: (1) boredom, and (2) loss of identity, meaning, engagement, and community.

Boredom

According to official statistics, people on average today spend nearly 40 hours per week at *paid* work, and in advanced economies slightly less.[5] Unpaid labor, such as personal housework or caring for children or pets,

---

[4] https://penguinrandomhousehighereducation.com/2018/05/21/steven-pinker-progress-ted-talk/.

[5] https://everhour.com/blog/average-working-hours/#:~:text=So%2C%20how%20many%20hours%20does,employees%20may%20work%20even%20less.

is, of course, not considered part of the working week. The Industrial Revolution made it possible to work year-round because very cold seasons did not prevent people from working, unlike their hunter-gatherer counterparts. Over the 20th century, due to government legislation, the average number of hours declined, e.g., in the US from nearly 60 to 40, thanks to the Fair Labor Standards Act. In spite of the decline, suffice it to say, working individuals spend a significant amount of their lifetime at work.

Viewed from the perspective that work is a bundle of activities, I have argued that technological change, which has been usurping human labor by technology, has reduced the need for human activity. Recently, Bill Gates, founder of Microsoft, has expressed the same sentiment; he has been quoted as saying, "Bill Gates believes Artificial Intelligence (AI) could shrink the workweek to just two or three days within the next decade."[6] If the need for human activity is reduced, then either the time would have to be filled, or individuals would have a pervasive sense of boredom.

A pervasive sense of boredom has consequences. None of us likes to be bored. Wilson *et al.* (2014) reported that in their study, 67% of men and 25% of women chose to give themselves an electric shock rather than be bored while sitting alone with their thoughts. Indeed, boredom has been linked to a wide variety of "bad" outcomes.[7] At the individual level, it may generate a range of psychological disorders (e.g., anger and aggression), behavioral problems (e.g., binge eating), and ailments (e.g., cholesterol levels). At the social and sociological levels, it can generate violence. See Box 1 for a list of the major consequences reported in scholarly literature.

---

[6]"Bill Gates believes artificial intelligence (AI) could shrink the workweek to just two or three days within the next decade."

Read more at: https://economictimes.indiatimes.com/news/international/global-trends/ai-will-cut-your-workweek-to-2-days-says-bill-gatesbut-warns-it-may-shrink-your-paycheck-too/articleshow/119611142.cms?utm_source=contentofinterest&utm_medium=text&utm_campaign=cppst.

[7]The following list is only a sample; for a fuller review of the benefits and problems of boredom, see Finkielsztein, M. (2023). The significance of boredom: A literature review. *Journal of Boredom Studies*, (1).

Box 1. Consequences of Boredom.

Boredom has been linked to a wide variety of "bad" outcomes.* At the individual level, it may generate the following:

1. Binge eating/overeating/polyphagia, i.e., eating more frequently and/or excessively than needed (Wemelsfelder, 1985).
2. Compulsive entertainment more frequently than individuals who are not bored (Martin, 2009).
3. A risk factor in heart disease (Franzmeier, quoted in Brisset and Snow, 1993) and high cholesterol levels.
4. Increase in the likelihood of dying (Britton and Shipley, 2010).
5. Many negative affective states, such as anger and aggression (Mercer-Lynn *et al.*, 2011, 2013; Rupp and Vodanovich, 1997; Van Tilburg *et al.*, 2019), depression (Farmer and Sundberg, 1986; Goldberg *et al.*, 2011; Malkovsky *et al.*, 2012; Newell *et al.*, 2012), anxiety (Fahlman *et al.*, 2009, 2013; Newell *et al.*, 2012), hostility (Dahlen *et al.*, 2004), hostility toward out-groups (Van Tilburg and Igou, 2011), loneliness (Farmer and Sundberg, 1986), and hopelessness.
6. Retreatism (understood as a state of psychic passivity (Misztal, 2016)), fatigue (Loukidou, 2008; Mann, 2016), and frustration (Baker *et al.*, 2010; Hill and Perkins, 1985).

At the social and sociological level, it may lead to the following:

1. Difficulty in long-lasting romantic relationships, relational problems, and divorces (Harasymchuk and Fehr, 2010).
2. Drawing adolescents into religious practices that advocate violence (e.g., Satanism [Clark, 1994]), delinquency and vandalism (Bengtsson, 2012; Csikszentmihalyi and Larson, 1978; Newberry and Duncan, 2001; Scitovsky, 1999), public violence and alcohol related assaults (Homel *et al.*, 1992), and murders.
3. 'Thrill killing,' premeditated murder motivated by the sheer excitement of the act (Branković, 2015).
4. Serving as a significant motivational factor in all kinds of violent and destructive behaviors, such as massacres (see the case of the My Lai Massacre in Maeland and Brunstad, 2009),

*The list below is only a sample, for a fuller view of the benefits and problems of boredom see, Finkielsztein (2023).

To be sure, boredom also has some positive effects: creativity, prosocial intentions, and time for reflection. Indeed, the leisure class is not uniformly bad; many of them espouse social causes and execute leadership functions. In fact, the French term, 'noblesse oblige,' which articulated the principle that with great wealth comes the responsibility (to give back to those who are less fortunate than oneself), could characterize some of the individuals Veblen referred to as belonging to the leisure class. They are active in the practical philanthropic landscape.

Loss of identity, meaning, community, and engagement

As I have noted in industrial societies, work has been a source of identity, meaning, community, and engagement. Simply put, identity refers to one's beliefs about oneself. Work provides meaning to individuals in a variety of ways. Work and work context also provide individuals with opportunities for community or contact with others, and keep many engaged. Social scientists have elaborated on each of these concepts, which themselves are closely related. For example, see Box 2 for a summary of the sources of identity.

Thus, a second consequence of the disappearance of work is the potential loss of meaning, identity, community, and engagement for many individuals. The literature (e.g., Bellah *et al.*, 1985; Wrzesniewski *et al.*, 1997) has identified three kinds of work orientations: job, career, and calling. In a nutshell, some people work for money, others for status and authority, and a third view work as a calling. Disappearance of work is going to be tough for all, especially for those classified as calling. What would a teacher do if she were replaced by an AI Program? I have already noted that work, as we know it, typically takes place in organizations, which offer numerous opportunities for contact with other human beings. By virtue of employment in organizations, employees are members of many groups and communities, such as teams, divisions, and professional networks (Rosso *et al.*, 2010). Organizations also provide community spaces for employees (Whyte, 1956; Levinson, 1965).

I summarized in Chapter 2 how the behaviors of Veblen's leisure class, those who are exempt from manual labor, serve to create and reinforce social stratification. They include vicarious leisure, conspicuous consumption, pecuniary emulation, maintaining elaborate standards of

Box 2. Mechanisms of meaning.[a]

1. Affirmation
   a. *Self-concordance*, or the degree to which people believe that they are behaving consistently with their values and interests.
   b. *Identity affirmation*, verification of valued self-identities through work.
   c. *Personal engagement*, where meaningfulness is derived from feeling personally immersed in the experience of working.

2. Self-efficacy
   a. *Personal control*
   b. *Competence*
   c. *Perceived impact*
3. *Self-esteem*, an individual's self-assessment of his /her own worth.
4. Purpose, a sense of directedness and intentionality in life.
5. *Belongingness*, a pervasive drive to form n maintain interpersonal relationships.[b]
6. *Transcendence*, connecting or superseding the ego to an entity greater than self or beyond.
7. *Cultural and interpersonal sensemaking*.[c]

[a]Rosso *et al.* (2010).
[b]We will deal with in the following section. It is included because this comes from the reference above.
[c]Same as footnote 3.

decency, and other behavior patterns identified by Veblen and elaborated by his followers. Almost all these behaviors serve to satisfy social psychological needs and are not easily explainable by economic logic. I am not classifying these behaviors as discontents, unlike the behaviors listed in Box 1.

Thus, a workless society not merely releases time but also shuts the door on many avenues for fulfilling social psychological needs. This societal transition is likely to demand significant adaptation by those accustomed to the industrial era work settings. Although our experience from the past (see Box 1) suggests several behavioral adaptation patterns by humans, newer options may arise for which there is no evidence for now.

There are also likely to be intergenerational differences in adaptation patterns: Coming generations, not handicapped by the assumptions of a work-based society or its behavioral patterns, may forge new paths for dealing with time and meeting their social psychological needs.

Scarcity Mindset

According to the Cambridge Dictionary, scarcity is "a situation in which something is not easy to find or get." The situation could be physical, i.e., due to objective factors, or cognitive, based on individual or collective beliefs and experiences, some inherited from the past. Hunter-gatherer communities, which relied on wild plants and animals for sustenance, suffered from a scarcity of food, which some claim limited their size. Agricultural societies had to contend with scarcity of water; scarcity has also been a fundamental problem in industrial societies, where raw materials were always limited. Scarcity generated a range of responses, both behavioral and psychological. Behaviorally, it may induce the acquisition of resources and hoarding of resources, or competitiveness. Cognitively, it also generated a scarcity mindset.[8]

Needless to say, over the history of humankind, humans were presented with a context of "objective" scarcity in many domains. There have been severe limitations on water, food, shelter, and other resources — all necessary for living. As sketched out in Figure 1, physical constraints in the 'objective' environment reinforced the human cognitive process to develop what I refer to here as the scarcity assumption, i.e., the assumption that resources in general are limited. This assumption generated not only behavioral responses such as hoarding but also led to competition for the scarce resource. No one competes for air for now, because it is generally deemed not to be scarce.[9] But that condition is not true for most resources.

---

[8] Scarcity mindset is a phrase coined by Mullainathan and Shafir (2013) who used the term in consumer psychology. I am borrowing their term, but I have imbued it with a slightly broader connotation.

[9] In an insightful observation, the Professor pointed out that oxygen or breathable air is not only increasingly scarce, but there is competition for non-polluted areas to live in all over the world.

The evolutionary experience of scarcity is reflected in human scholarly pursuits, primarily in economics, psychology, and sociology, all related to business. Scarcity is a key concept in these fields. Economics is often dubbed the 'dismal science,' because a substantial portion of economics is focused on decision-making under *resource constraints*. Indeed, concepts like opportunity costs and price mechanisms that animate scholarly discourses on decision making imply scarce resources, be they physical or cognitive. Economists link scarcity to value: the scarcer an input, the more valuable it is.[10] In psychology, scarcity is viewed as a mindset that views resources, opportunities, and even relationships as limited, leading to feelings of competition and fear of loss. (e.g., Covey, 2020). Much like economists, sociologists refer to scarcity as the fundamental economic problem of limited resources and unlimited human wants; but according to sociologists, unlike economists, the scarcity mindset leads to competition and social inequalities as individuals and groups strive to access and control scarce resources.

So, what does the scarcity mindset have to do with a workless society? Recall that a workless society, a society where normal work activities can be fully automated, is a possibility that can be *imagined*, but it is not one with enormous physical evidence. It is presented in opposition to the pervasive assumption that work is ubiquitous. Only Veblen has posited an antonym to the working class — the leisure class, whose pursuits are not intended to satisfy their lower-level needs of food, shelter, and clothing. A workless society has to contend with a situation where lower-level human needs are fully met for most of the population. In other words, in this kind of society, there is enough food, shelter, and clothing to go around for all.

In order to take human physical life out of the grip of economic calculus, workless societies are forced to shed the assumption of a scarcity mindset, at least in the realm of basic human necessities. But before I go further, I want to focus on another barrier to the assumption: the human need for control, which gets intertwined with a scarcity mindset in many policy debates.

[10] In the case of oxygen, my earlier example, because it is not scarce, its economic value is almost non-existent.

Human Need for Control

The need for power is one of the human characteristics. Power is one of the three primary human needs identified by psychologists, e.g., David McClelland,[11] in developing his Thematic Apperception Test (TAT).[12] As observed by McClelland and his followers, individuals with a high need for power seek to shape the actions and decisions of others and are often drawn to positions where they can lead and direct others. They enjoy competition and often strive to win arguments or debates; they value status, recognition, and a high reputation; they often have a need for personal prestige and a better personal status.

Scholars hold widely differing views on power. Psychologists generally hold a negative view of power. For example, Adler is quoted to have said, "The striving for personal power is a disastrous delusion and poisons man's living together. Whoever desires the human community must renounce the striving for power over others."[13] Even McClelland wanted to train people to be achievement-oriented but not power-oriented. Sociologists and economists, on the other hand, were more comfortable dealing with power, partly because they were focused on action at the macro-levels: societal (sociologists) or pricing actions in the industry (economists). Psychologists, economists, and sociologists all *agree* that the desire to control others is a common expression of the need for power.

---

[11] Henry A. Murray (1893–1988) was arguably the first psychologist to create a catalogue of human needs, having about 20 of them, including needs for order, recognition, nurturance, dominance, and autonomy (Murray, 1938). David McClelland was a student of Murray's and built on his work. He created a three-category system of needs — achievement (nAch), affiliation (nAff), and power (nPow), and embedded these three needs within a general theory of motivation (McClelland, 1965). The need for affiliation is the motivation to establish and maintain friendly relationships with others; the need for power is the need to control and influence the behavior of others, and the need for achievement is the need to demonstrate high performance levels and high standards of excellence. In contrast to Maslow and Alderfer, McClelland believed that needs are learned and can be developed through training.

[12] *TAT*: The Thematic Apperception Test (TAT) is a projective psychological test developed by Henry Murray and Christiana Morgan in the 1930s. It asks individuals to create stories about ambiguous images, revealing their underlying motives, concerns, and social perceptions.

[13] http://www.adlerian.us/qu-power.htm#:~:text=Alfred%20Adler%3A,many%20as%20an%20obvious%20thought.

Stepping aside moral judgments, control is an essential principle in today's organizations, where most work is carried out. Hierarchical organizations are built on the concept of authority, a form of power. The concept of authority is useful because, among many things, it enables relatively quick allocation of scarce resources at various organizational levels. It also constrains human behavior in the workplace. As I mentioned in Chapter 3, some job design theorists put human autonomy as an objective in an organization, trying to protect workers from 'oppressive' authority. Control is exercised not merely at the micro job design level, but at macro levels where policies regarding jobs are also conceived. Laws in the workplace are designed to curtail the power of the employer for the benefit of workers.

A recent example in the US highlights the need for control in organizations. Amid the coronavirus pandemic four years ago, the country shut down and changed how Americans do their jobs. According to the American Community Survey (ACS), remote work increased dramatically across all major industries between 2019 and 2021. Pew reported that nearly 2 years into the COVID-19 pandemic, roughly 6-in-10 US workers who say their jobs can mainly be done from home (59%) are working from home all or most of the time.[14] However, the need for organizational control asserted itself: For example, Forbes reported that J.P. Morgan CEO Jamie Dimon made it clear that:

> Employees need to be on campus, and they need to see what their fellow employees are doing each day as a way of helping to expand the reach of the business they're in. If everyone's somewhere else and only expected to show up presentably on Zoom (Dimon notes that employees don't pay attention on Zoom like they do when in the office), they and shareholders will be denied the growth that can only come from smart, energetic people improving one another by working with one another[15].

To imagine a workless society is to confront the tight grip of the two interlinked forces: scarcity mindset and desire for control. And because they are supported by human needs and our own ecological experience,

---

[14] Pew: https://www.gwi.com/blog/working-from-home-vs-office#:~:text=While%20working%20in%20the%20office,best%20of%20both%20worlds%20together.

[15] https://www.forbes.com/sites/johntamny/2025/02/23/jamie-dimon-is-right-remote-work-is-a-waste-of-time-and-talent/.

they will erect significant *cognitive* barriers. As noted in Chapter 1, these barriers could be religious ("Work is worship"), psychology-related ("Lieben und arbeiten"), and identity-related ("Work is the core of identity"). And a catalogue of others. One of the most recently invoked arguments is the *Jevons* paradox: the idea that an increase in efficiency in resource use will generate an increase in resource consumption rather than a decrease.[16] Thus, as the sources of material comfort become plentiful, their demand will increase, the corollary being that the assumption of a workless society is absurd.

Scarcity, Control, and Workless Society

As a mode of social stratification, Veblen's leisure class can exist only in the presence of *actual* material scarcity. Technological advances may eviscerate scarcity in most material matters, but not the *human* experience of scarcity. For Veblen's leisure class, exemption from manual labor also served as a status symbol and thus a means of control. Indeed, technology is not likely to eradicate stratification. While I do not want to speculate what forms of stratification are likely to develop, Veblen himself has suggested, perhaps unwittingly, a way in which status distinctions can sustain themselves, with his enigmatic notion of vicarious leisure, leisure enjoyed through the labor of others. Here, the need for control for some takes the form of lording over others, simply because such lording is intrinsically satisfying.

Thus, although the actual scarcity in material things may be made to disappear, beliefs about material scarcity (scarcity mindset) and beliefs about an appropriate form of social control are likely to persist.

[16]In 1865, the English economist William Stanley Jevons observed that technological improvements that increased the efficiency of coal use led to the increased consumption of coal in a wide range of industries. He argued that, contrary to common intuition, technological progress could not be relied upon to reduce fuel consumption (Wikipedia) (https://en.wikipedia.org/wiki/Jevons_paradox. Indeed, it has become fashionable to invoke this paradox. For example, "Jevons paradox strikes again!" Microsoft CEO Satya Nadella wrote on social media in the wake of the DeepSeek announcement. "As AI gets more efficient and accessible, we will see its use skyrocket, turning it into a commodity we just can't get enough of." (https://news.northeastern.edu/2025/02/07/jevons-paradox-ai-future/.)

Beliefs about material scarcity: Scarcity mindset refers to our *beliefs*, not to the possibility or even the actuality of abundance. Thus, although the actual scarcity in material things may be made to disappear, the scarcity mindset among humans is likely to persist. Human beings *genuinely* differ on whether there are enough resources in the world for everyone. Indeed, I have earlier noted that almost all of our academic enterprises are underpinned by an assumption of scarcity. These deeply held beliefs mask the possibility of a workless universe opened up by technological developments. Hence, unlike in the case of air, there must be some degree of control on how resource allocation decisions are made.

Beliefs about control: This desire for power and control is built into the human character. Because the strength of the desire is not uniformly distributed among human things, policy debates pertaining to the context of work tend to be dictated by the more vocal ones. Our beliefs about the appropriate form of social control typically divide most *vocal* disputants in policy debates into opposing camps, with one camp strongly holding onto beliefs about social justice, with its populist versions engaged in advocacy of social justice, and the other upholding an efficient allocation of scarce resources, favoring meritocracy of various kinds.

The possibility of a workless society hinges upon technological developments eradicating *material* scarcity. However, just as in the case of our belief about a geocentric world, technological development may only marginally change our beliefs in the beginning and then too slowly later on. Also, these developments certainly do not address our need for control.

For analytic purposes, the two beliefs — about scarcity mindset and mode of control — can be juxtaposed to yield four different scenarios of how the context of work is shaped. This is pictorially presented in Figure 1. One could conjecture four different types of control regimes: manufactured scarcity, selective scarcity, aristocracy, and a utopian regime. The first three regimes tend to be plutocratic, with control resting in the hands of a few (no surprise there).

1. *Manufactured scarcity*: In these regimes, the possibilities opened up by technology are constrained, real scarcity is eradicated, but scarcity is maintained by those in control — the ruling elite, to control the population at large. These regimes may resemble feudalism of the past, with society being composed of a system of lords and serfs.

2. *Selective scarcity*: Here, the attention of those in control is to harness the energies of the population at large for what *they* deem to be noble purposes. Thus, those in control determine the membership of individuals in ambitious undertakings, just as the leisure class in their pursuit of conspicuous consumption erected barriers to entry. The 'ambitious undertakings' in the current circumstances could be space travel, global warming, or something else. The difference between the two regimes, this and the previous, is the sphere in which control is exercised: In the regime of manufactured scarcity, material scarcity is used as a tool for control, whereas in selective scarcity, material prosperity is more or less assured, but participation in 'noble ventures' is not.
3. *Aristocratic regimes*: In these regimes, a workless society is understood and accepted as a reality, but social control is still exercised. The bases of control are not the ability to withhold material resources or limit membership as in the previous two regimes, but social psychological factors, including individuals' birthright or characteristics. The Indian caste system, although it arose not in abundance but in scarcity, may offer a starting point for postulating some characteristics of these regimes. Individuals rely on referent power (French and Raven, 1959) to exercise control in society. Put another way, the basis of control shifts from control of material resources to sociological factors.
4. *Utopian regimes*: These regimes neither dwell on control of material resources nor on bases rooted in other factors.

As laid out in Table 1, we can array the four societal arrangements according to the beliefs animating them. A key insight from the analysis of a workless society is that the above-mentioned two distinct beliefs *may at times generate policy prescriptions that may appear similar*, but they

Table 1. Beliefs and Regimes.

	Beliefs about scarcity	
	REAL	**NOT REAL**
Exercise of control	Manufactured scarcity	Aristocracy
	Selective scarcity	Utopian

operate from different impulses. In the next chapter, I will examine three policy proposals in the US, both to indicate the pervasiveness of the scarcity assumption and to show how the aforementioned two beliefs, though distinct, may generate some very similar policy alternatives.

References

Baker, R., D'Mello, S., Rodrigo, M. M., and Graesser, A. (2010). Better to Be Frustrated than Bored: The Incidence, Persistence, and Impact of Learners' Cognitive-Affective States During Interactions with Three Different Computer-Based Learning Environments. *International Journal of Human Computer Studies*, 68(4), 223–241.

Bellah, R. N., Madsen, R., Sullivan, W. M., Swidler, A., and Tipton, S. M. (1985). Habits of the heart. Berkeley: University of California Press.

Bengtsson, T. (2012). Boredom and Action—Experiences from Youth Confinement. *Journal of Contemporary Ethnography*, 41(5), 526–553.

Branković, S. (2015). Boredom, Dopamin, and the Thrill of Psychosis: Psychiatry in a New Key. *Psychiatria Danubina*, 27(2), 126–137.

Brisset, D. and Snow, R. (1993). Boredom: Where the Future Isn't. *Symbolic Interaction*, 16(3), 237–256.

Britton, A. and Shipley, M. J. (2010). Bored to Death? *International Journal of Epidemiology*, 39(2), 370–371.

Clark, C. (1994). Clinical Assessment of Adolescents Involved in Satanism. *Adolescence*, 29(114), 461–468.

Covey, S. R. (2020). *The 7 Habits of Highly Effective People*. Simon & Schuster.

Csikszentmihalyi, M. and Larson, R. (1978). Intrinsic Rewards in School Crime. *Crime & Delinquency*, 24(3), 321–335.

Dahlen, E., Martin, R., Ragan, K., and Kuhlman, M. (2004). Boredom Proneness in Anger and Aggression: Effects of Impulsiveness and Sensation Seeking. *Personality and Individual Differences*, 37, 1615–1627.

Fahlman, S., Mercer, K., Gaskovski, P., Eastwood, A., and Eastwood, J. (2009). Does a Lack of Life Meaning Cause Boredom? Results from Psychometric, Longitudinal, and Experimental Analyses. *Journal of Social and Clinical Psychology*, 28(3), 307–340.

Fahlman, S., Mercer-Lynn, K., Flora, D., and Eastwood, J. (2013). Development and Validation of the Multidimensional State Boredom Scale. *Assessment*, 20(1), 68–85.

Farmer, R. and Sundberg, N. (1986). Boredom Proneness — The Development and Correlates of a New Scale. *Journal of Personality Assessment*, 50(1), 4–17.

Finkielsztein, M. (2023). The Significance of Boredom: A Literature Review. *Journal of Boredom Studies*, 1.

French, J. and Raven, B. (1959). The Bases of Social Power. In Cartwright, D. Ed., *Studies in Social Power*, pp. 150–167. Ann Arbor, MI: Institute for Social Research.

Goldberg, Y., Eastwood, J., Laguardia, J., and Danckert, J. (2011). Boredom: An Emotional Experience Distinct from Apathy, Anhedonia, or Depression. *Journal of Social and Clinical Psychology*, 30(6), 647–666.

Harasymchuk, C. and Fehr, B. (2010). A Script Analysis of Relational Boredom: Causes, Feelings, and Coping Strategies. *Journal of Social and Clinical Psychology*, 29(9), 988–1019.

Hill, A. B. and Perkins, R. E. (1985). Towards a Model of Boredom. *British Journal of Psychology*, 76, 235–240.

Homel, R., Tomsen, S., and Thommeny, J. (1992). Public Drinking and Violence: Not Just an Alcohol Problem. *Journal of Drug Issues*, 22(3), 679–697.

Levinson, H. (1965). Reciprocation: The relationship between man and organization. *Administrative Science Quarterly*, 9(4), 370–390.

Loukidou, E. (2008). Boredom in the Workplace: A Qualitative Study of Psychiatric Nurses in Greece. PhD Thesis, Loughborough University.

Madsen, R., Sullivan, W. M., Swidler, A., and Tipton, S. M. (1985). Habits of the Heart. *Individualism and Commitment in American Life.*

Maeland, B. and Brunstad, P. O. (2009). *Enduring Military Boredom. From 1750 to the Present*. Palgrave Macmillan.

Malkovsky, E., Merrifield, C., Goldberg, Y., and Danckert, J. (2012). Exploring the Relationship Between Boredom and Sustained Attention. *Experimental Brain Research*, 221(1), 59–67.

Mann, S. (2016). *The Upside of Downtime. Why Boredom is Good.* Robinson.

Martin, P. (2009). *Sex, Drugs and Chocolate: The Science of Pleasure*. Harper Collins.

Mercer-Lynn, K., Flora, D., Fahlman, S., and Eastwood, J. (2011). The Measurement of Boredom: Differences Between Existing Self-Report Scales. *Assessment*, 20(5), 585–596.

Mercer-Lynn, K., Hunter, J., and Eastwood, J. (2013). Is Trait Boredom Redundant? *Journal of Social and Clinical Psychology*, 32(8), 897–916.

Misztal, B. (2016). The Ambiguity of Everyday Experience: Between Normality and Boredom. *Qualitative Sociology Review*, 12(4), 100–119.

Murray, H. A. (1937). Facts which support the concept of need or drive. *The Journal of psychology*, 3(1), 27–42.

Newberry, A. and Duncan, R. (2001). Roles of Boredom and Life Goals in Juvenile Delinquency. *Journal of Applied Social Psychology*, 31, 527–541.

Newell, S., Harries, P., and Ayers, S. (2012). Boredom Proneness in a Psychiatric Inpatient Population. *The International Journal of Social Psychiatry*, 58(5), 488–495.

Rosso, B. D., Dekas, K. H., and Wrzesniewski, A. (2010). On the meaning of work: Theoretical integration and review. *Research in organizational behavior*, 30, 91–127.

Rupp, D. and Vodanovich, S. (1997). The Role of Boredom Proneness in Self-Reported Anger and Aggression. *Journal of Social Behavior & Personality*, 12(4), 925–936.

Scitovsky, T. (1999). Boredom — An Overlooked Disease? *Challenge*, 42(5), 5–15.

The Economist (2025). *The New Inheritocracy*, p. 10. March 1–7, 2025.

Van Tilburg, W., Igou, E., Maher, P., and Lennon, J. (2019). Various Forms of Existential Distress Are Associated with Aggressive Tendencies. *Personality and Individual Differences*, 144, 111–119.

Van Tilburg, W. and Igou, E. (2011). On Boredom and Social Identity: A Pragmatic Meaning-Regulation Approach. *Personality and Social Psychology Bulletin*, 37(12), 1679–1691.

Wemelsfelder, F. (1985). Animal Boredom: Is a Scientific Study of the Subjective Experiences of Animals Possible? In *Advances in Animal Welfare Science 1984* (pp. 115–154). Martinus Nijhoff Publishers.

Westgate, E. C. and Steidle, B. (2020). Lost by definition: Why boredom matters for psychology and society. *Social and Personality Psychology Compass*, 14(11), e12562.

Whyte, W. H. (1956) *The Organization Man*. New York: Simon & Schuster.

Wrzesniewski, A., Dekas K., and Roiss B. (2009). Calling, In S.J. Lopez, and A. Beauchamps (Eds.) *The Encyclopedia of Positive Psychology*, pp. 115–118.

Chapter 9

Workless Society and Blindness of Public Policy

Abstract

The ubiquity of work is built into our mindset that we often overlook the possibility of a workless society being thrust upon us by technological development. To illustrate this point, I touch upon three policy debates that have animated US politics recently: minimum wage, health care, and universal basic income, which received a boost because of the sponsorship of well-known political figures.

In the previous chapters, I have laid out the argument that technology development, especially in AI, has brought us to the doorstep of a workless society, but noted that the ubiquity of work remains a tacit yet central assumption of our policy discussions. Thus, the possibilities — both opportunities and challenges — opened up by imagining a workless society do not get a hearing in policy deliberations.

The assumption of ubiquity of work underpins numerous policies, but I will illustrate the pervasiveness of the assumption with three examples. My choice is guided by two *specific* criteria: first, the issue is not too complex to understand,[1] and second, its relationship to work is too

[1] The three policies — minimum wage, access to health care, and universal basic income — have strong technical components, but in my judgment, the polices themselves are easier to comprehend than others, such as nuclear deterrence, which may require a sophisticated understanding of the technology.

obvious to merit pointing out in detail. The minimum wage, access to health care, and the universal basic income have all been debated in the US news lately, thanks to the advocacy of influential and well-known politicians. My intent here is not to detail the technical details of the evidence — including what academic scholarship has to say — but to relate the issue to the ubiquity of work, scarcity, and control that arise from it (as I noted in the previous chapter).

The chapter is organized as follows. In three successive sections, I touch upon minimum wage laws, health care, and universal basic income, confining myself to issues that I deem relevant to the argument about a workless society. In the final section, I suggest how these issues can be interpreted from the point of workless society, setting the stage for the final chapter.

Minimum Wage[2]

Minimum wage refers to the floor of a price floor on wages, ensuring that workers receive a certain level of compensation. This is not to be confused with a living wage, which, in its simplest, is what an individual, one full-time worker, must earn on an hourly basis to help cover the cost of their family's minimum basic needs where they live while still being self-sufficient.

Minimum wage laws refer to the measures governments have made to introduce, monitor, and enforce a minimum wage. These laws appear to have had universal appeal. First introduced perhaps in New Zealand, the minimum wage policy was adopted by many other countries, including Australia, the United Kingdom, Latin America, and the European Union. In the US, the minimum wage was established as a federal policy in the Fair Labor Standards Act of 1938 (FLSA). In the third chapter, I referred to FLSA as one of the means to control the *context* of work. The original bill set a wage floor, instituted a 44-hour work week, and protected children from prematurely entering the workforce. Since 1938, the FLSA has been amended multiple times, with added exemptions and expansions.

---

[2] There are eight basic needs — food, childcare, health care, housing, transportation, civic engagement, broadband, and other necessities — that make up the cost components of the living wage, with an additional cost associated with income and payroll taxes. https://livingwage.mit.edu/pages/methodology.

The latest proposed changes in Congress — the Raise the Wage Act of 2023 — would increase the federal minimum wage to $17 per hour.

Minimum wage laws have been a topic of perennial debate in the US, where there have been voices *against* and *for* minimum wage laws. The Cato Institute[3] has provided four major reasons why minimum wage laws have negative consequences: (1) it would result in job losses; (2) it would hurt low-skilled workers; (3) it would have a limited effect on reducing poverty, and (4) it would have negative consequences for consumers. During the last decade, Senator Bernie Sanders has been a major proponent *for* raising the minimum wage in the US. Although the rising income inequality in the US has been a factor, Sanders has also made the argument:

> The $7.25 an hour minimum wage is a starvation wage. It must be raised to a living wage — at least $17 an hour. In the year 2025, a job should lift you out of poverty, not keep you in it. At a time of massive income and wealth inequality, we can no longer tolerate millions of workers trying to survive on just $10 or $12 an hour.[4]

It is easy to see that the assumption of a workless society renders the minimum wage laws irrelevant. In the US, the assumption may nullify the very need for the Department of Labor, which was created in 1913 for promoting the welfare of workers. The laws may be well-intended and address the power imbalance in the negotiation and bargaining between the managerial class and "employees," but they clearly are rooted in a vision of society where work is central to meeting the needs of people.

Access to Health Care

How are health care and a workless society related? Although on the surface the question itself may sound odd, technological advancement interlinks the health care system and workless society in two major ways:

---

[3] chrome-extension://efaidnbmnnnibpcajpcglclefindmkaj/https://www.cato.org/sites/cato.org/files/four_reasons_not_to_raise_the_minimum_wage.pdf.

[4] https://www.sanders.senate.gov/press-releases/news-sanders-scott-174-colleagues-introduce-bill-to-raise-minimum-wage-to-17-by-2030-benefitting-nearly-22-million-americans/.

Health care as a cluster of related activities, and the health care system as the output of societal architecture.

If healthcare is viewed as work, a set of activities that include the work of all health care professionals — nursing staff, doctors or surgeons — we can visualize them as pervious to automation. The application of Artificial Intelligence (AI) in health care is not new; for example, MYCIN and CADUCEUS were expert systems developed in the 1970s for diagnostic effectiveness. More recently, AI has helped to streamline healthcare operations. This seemed to have resulted in lower operational costs, reduced staff burnout, enhanced patient experience, ensured data privacy and compliance, and improved data access and transfer.[5] But in the coming waves, much of the professional work is likely to be automated. Recall what Bill Gates had opined: that teachers and doctors are likely to be disrupted by AI (see previous chapter). Technological advancements have a *universal* quality: They disrupt specific activities wherever they are in the world.

The actual delivery of health care to a patient is, however, dependent on the specific systems developed. Unlike the universality of diagnostic activities, health care systems and laws *vary* significantly across countries. For example, Brazil and Norway offer free health care for all its citizens; some countries like Canada, France, Germany, and the UK also have universal health coverage; Singapore is often ranked at top of the world's health and health systems, followed by Japan and South Korea and the US health care system is a mixed system of public and private financing, with no universal health care.

As in the case of the minimum wage law before, I will restrict myself to the US, without reproducing the ideological debates or scholarly treatises on the US Health Care System. In the US, regulations over the years have created a *link* between health care and work. This history goes back to before the Great Depression, with several efforts by the government to enact legislation failing before and for some years following the depression.[6] However, during the 1960s, employer-based health coverage grew (and was found to be excluded from an employee's taxable income), and in 1965, a year after the passing of the Civil Rights Act, the Medicare and

[5] KMS Health care, https://kms-healthcare.com/blog/automation-in-healthcare/#:~:text=with%20KMS%20Healthcare-,What%20Does%20Automation%20in%20Healthcare%20Mean?,in%20helping%20healthcare%20organizations%20scale.

[6] For a non-technical history, see https://pmc.ncbi.nlm.nih.gov/articles/PMC10810293/.

Medicaid programs were incorporated into the Social Security Act, which was tied to the workplace, and signed into law by President Johnson. The bill had massive public approval, the support of the hospital and insurance industries.

Thus, one crucial aspect of the US system is that a significant number of individuals have their health care tied to their workplace. Remember though that was a policy choice. A workless society, however, breaks the association between health care and work. Perhaps more important is the prediction (See Bill Gates' reference above) that most of health care-related activity can be automated. In other words, an individual does not have to rely on other individuals or workplaces to receive health care.

This may seem odd, but the possibility is now on the horizon. It is not necessary to view health care through the prism of scarcity, and the need for social control is not necessary under the assumption of a workless society.

Universal Basic Income

Universal basic income (UBI) is the concept that all citizens of a given population regularly receive a minimum income without a means test or need to perform work. This is different from a guaranteed minimum income is paid only to those who do not already receive an income that is enough to live on. A UBI would be received independently of any other income.

Unlike minimum wage or health care policy, no country has to date promulgated a full universal basic income. But it is not a new idea. In the nomadic, hunting, and gathering societies all land was treated as *commons*. That is, everyone can forage on the land, but no one can own it. A similar right to use of land has existed in many small-scale agrarian communities right up to the 20th century. According to Widerquist (2024),[7] the connection between common land and UBI is that both institutions allow every individual to have access to the resources they need to survive without conditions imposed by others.

The concept of a basic income guarantee has experienced three distinct waves of support (Weiderquist, 2024): (1) from 1910 to 1940, (2) 1960s and 1970s, (3) 2010s. By far the largest wave of support began

[7] Widerquist, K. (2024). *Universal Basic Income*. MIT Press.

to take off in the early 2010s, and it has increased every year since then. Recently, it has received support from unlikely quarters. For one, Andrew Yang[8], a Democratic US politician, started advocating the idea. For another, Elon Musk argued that UBI is inevitable. In his eyes, "advances in AI will change the world to the point that eventually, hardly anyone will even have a job; this will require governments to pay out a universal basic income, as most people won't even be paying a paycheck."[9]

To be sure, in spite of the similarity of their expected outcomes, there are differences among the proponents of UBI. Individuals like Musk view UBI as the natural endgame for technological progress; we could call them techno determinists. Techno determinists foresee the disappearance of work, as all work gets automated; they understand the emergence of a workless society. For others, UBI is necessary to restrain the widening income inequality, for still others, it is to make living possible for the indigent. We could call them redistributionists. Redistributionists do not address technological change, but as policy wonks, they are concerned with the impending loss of employment for many and the heightening of income inequality.

The Stranglehold of Assumptions

The assumption of ubiquity of work and its correlates, scarcity mindset, and nature of control, are visible in the aforementioned three examples. Let me briefly illustrate:

Minimum wage laws: The case of the minimum wage laws is the easiest to analyze. As I had mentioned, the laws arose during the industrial era, when "work" as we know it today came into existence. These laws were intended to be a solution to the unbridled power of capital over labor, primarily in capitalist economies. Both kinds of economists, Capitalist and Marxian, bought into the notion that for most of the population, *work is necessary for subsistence*. This ubiquity of work is thus built into their reasoning. Thus, these laws reflect a belief in scarcity as a fundamental

---

[8]Andrew Yang gained mainstream attention as a candidate in the 2020 Democratic Party presidential primaries. His signature policy, a monthly universal basic income (UBI) of $1,000, was intended to offset job displacement by automation. In 2021, he founded the political party and action committee Forward Party, for which he serves as co-chair alongside former New Jersey Governor Christine Todd Whitman and Michael S. Willner.

[9]https://finance.yahoo.com/news/elon-musk-says-universal-income-100212824.html.

characteristic of our material life. The laws explicitly utilize the coercive power of the state to control the labor management negotiations by placing a floor on wages to protect labor.

The contemporary discussion of these laws continues to be mired in the assumption of the ubiquity of work. Thus, the newer versions of automation — AI, for example — are viewed as generating decision options which oscillate between efficiency and wages, but the emancipation possibilities of technology do not register on the discursive radar.

Access to health care: As I have summarized earlier, health care in the US involves both (a) the actual activities involved in diagnosis, care, and prevention, and (b) the delivery of services that include government control and health insurance. Recent advances make it feasible to automate actual activities, and the possibility of personalized medicine looms large on the horizon. Although the exact timing of the availability of personalized medicine can be debated, as Gates' opinion (referred to earlier) suggests that techno optimists converge on the possibility of fully automated and personalized medicine.

So, what is this fuss about? The issue is complex, but in order to bring the discussion to the context of a workless society, I will first touch upon two related issues. First, in a workless society, the link between health care and jobs loses its relevance. The basic contract, "If you have a job, you have health care," makes limited sense if human beings are freed from work. Second, we should in the near term expect the AI-related innovations to course the health insurance industry, offering efficiencies we could not have imagined even a few years ago.

Even if impending automation frees health care from the clasp of scarcity mindset and makes universal health care feasible, the issue is probably not likely to be resolved. We have arguments being marshaled on both sides: for and against universal health care.[10] The critical issue in a workless society would not be the feasibility but the *desirability* of the principle. Put another way, how do we control access to health care? The control could be in the hands of an individual (in the case of autocracy), a group (in the case of oligarchy), or even a process (e.g., democracy).

Universal basic income: The techno-optimist version of universal basic income acknowledges the emergence of a workless society and proposes

[10] For an example of the arguments, see https://pmc.ncbi.nlm.nih.gov/articles/PMC4940671/.

Table 1. Assumptions in the three examples.

Examples Assumptions	Minimum Age	Access to Health Care	Universal Basic Income
Concern about technological development	Unemployment	System efficiency; Accuracy of diagnosis and health care	Workless society
Work	Necessary	Health care links	May not be necessary
Scarcity	Present	Present	Present
Control	Regulation of the unchecked power of capital	Equitable rationing of health care	Blunt the economic impact of automation

Source: Widerquist (2024). *Universal Basic Income*. MIT Press.

UBI as a remedy to the widespread unemployment they fear. Redistributionists do not recognize the impending technological disruption, but for them. UBI is a way to battle extreme poverty, with UBI offering a floor level of income to all. They are thus captured by a scarcity mindset, but advanced regulatory control as an antidote to the excesses of income inequality.

Thus, just as in the case of health care, UBI proponents do not address the control issue: Why should there be any control of material resources when we may be moving into a time period in society where material scarcity is a thing of the past?

In Table 1, I have summarized the three options along the critical dimensions of interest to this book.

Conclusion

In this chapter, I have striven to show that many well-meaning policy prescriptions, even those lauded as liberal and humanistic, are infected with the assumptions of scarcity and control, whose utility may have been thwarted by technological, development.

Chapter 10

Revisiting the Assumption of a Workless Society

Abstract

In this chapter, I revisit the assumption of a workless society in an attempt to outline the practical implications of the assumption. The simple answer to the question, "So what?" is the possibility that a shift in assumptions can open up a new set of options for us to consider. But an assumption being a cognitive assertion, its translation to practical matters will take time and, more importantly, a set of pragmatic moves at the collective level. I will sketch a set of issues that need to be confronted in order for the idea of a workerless society to move from imagination to practice.

The possibility of a workless society outlined in this book is built on the assumption that work as we conceive of it today is a cluster of activities, and that those activities currently conducted by human effort, both manual and mental, can more or less be fully automated. This assumption and the twin pillars of scarcity mindset and need for human control are likely to invoke both excitement and fear in different sectors of the global population. At the moment, the fear appears to be the most vocal response, but we have also heard some early musings from those who are excited by the possibility. The debate between the two groups is likely to grow in intensity.

Seemingly new assumptions are rightfully challenged in the beginning. Many a time, the challenges are based on misconceptions, but the challenges could also be due to pragmatic reasons. The sociopolitical context typically plays a central role in pragmatic decisions, and a workless society is not likely to be any exception. As I have maintained in this book, although the possibility of a workless society is opened up by technological development, the social arrangements we settle upon are not dictated by technology alone. In this chapter, I not only try to dispel some misconceptions about a workless society, but step back from the major premise and ruminate upon a select set of issues raised by the possibility.

Misconceptions About a Workless Society

In the beginning, I want to address three *potential* misconceptions that have formed around the assumption of a workless society presented in the book: workless society as a new idea, technological determinism, and human motivation.

Workless society as a new idea

This book makes the critical observation that our conception of work has been evolving over the years, and as Lucassen's model demonstrated, our current conception of work arose in the wake of the Industrial Revolution, when a vast number of individuals began to work in factories, moving away from their agrarian roots. In this conception of work, individuals exchanged labor for remuneration, and over time, for most individuals, work was necessary to meet their lower-level needs.[1]

But a visible number of individuals did *not* have to work as per Thorstein Veblen's *Leisure Class*. Veblen's insight was that during the Gilded Age, a class of individuals, by virtue of the vast wealth they had accumulated, did not have to work. This leisure class behaved somewhat differently: they engaged in conspicuous consumption patterns (as per Veblen), and their lifestyle in general was different from that of the working class. Veblen also noted that the leisure class viewed the proletariat with *disdain*; in their eyes, anyone who had to work belonged to the lower echelons of the society. One could suggest that a workless society existed

[1] Lower-level needs, as Abraham Maslow would have characterized them.

even during the Gilded Age, but that it was confined to the upper economic echelons of the society.

In today's world, we have witnessed another phenomenon: the rise of trust fund "babies." The term "trust fund baby" refers to a person who benefits financially from a trust fund, typically established by their parents or guardians to provide financial security. The term itself was coined around the 1970s. Trusts can be for anyone, like kids or certain people, giving control over how the money is used. Some trust fund babies live a life of luxury, but not all trust funds belong to super-rich families. The term, however, often carries a *negative* connotation, suggesting a lack of work ethic or reliance on inherited wealth. The term "trust fund baby" often brings to mind young people living in luxury with no money worries. One could argue that trust fund babies who do not have to work form another member of the workless society.

Thus, the phenomenon of a workless society has existed for a long time. So then, what is the difference? I can identify two major points of difference. First, the assumption of a workless society addresses a situation where *few* need to work, unlike the leisure class elites or trust fund babies of today. So, this assumption implies a society where worklessness is the *norm, not the exception*. Second, and related to the first, worklessness is thus neither confined to economic elites nor does it refer to a pejorative term.

Thus, worklessness itself is not new, but its character has changed.

Technological determinism

The assumption of a workless society advanced in the book is based on a conception of work as a set of activities and does not address the meaning, engagement, and the sense of community that work and the workplace bring to an individual. The key argument is that successive waves of automation — robotics, digitalization, and now Artificial Intelligence have eviscerated the need for human intervention in the workplace, and humans may not be needed for Talcott Parsons' technical and managerial levels. Yes, technological advances will continue to exert an *enormous* influence on this evolution.

I have already noted that we can identify at least two groups of UBI advocates, those who understand the progress of technology like Elon Musk and those like Andrew Yang, who are guided by a sense of social justice. We do not know how society itself will evolve to deal with worklessness because that evolution is the result of a collective process. Indeed, our scarcity mindset and the need for control will play a role in that evolution. A collective process can halt the progress of technological development or the diffusion of technology. I do not have concrete instances, but this possibility has already been foreseen in the science fiction series *Dune* by Frank Herbert:

> Thou shalt not make a machine in the likeness of a man's mind" Paul quoted. Once men turned their thinking over to machines in the hope that this would set them free. But that only permitted other men with machines to enslave them.

The prohibition against creating machines in the likeness of man was a political (collective) decision in the Sci-Fi series. This is only one scenario. Alternatively, society could evolve into a world of manufactured scarcity or oligarchy as identified in Chapter 8.

Thus, whereas work itself is likely to be automated and is thus dependent on technological development, what form society will take is going to be determined by sociopolitical forces, and not merely dictated by technological developments.

Human motivation

A third misconception about a workless society is the *absence* of incentives for human beings to engage in any activity. Why should human beings do any work if they are not incentivized? The question itself is rooted in the assumption of an industrial age workplace, recognizing only the economic character of any individual. This concept of incentives holds up the image of an individual having to be enticed to work, with money as the major form of incentive being dangled in front of her.

It is likely that a workless society will most likely eliminate the influence of monetary incentives. However, as Lucassen has demonstrated, prior to the industrial era, humans engaged in activities, but the monetary system we take for granted today did not then exist. Indeed, the proverb, "Man does not live by bread alone," has been with us since Biblical times. Maslow provided us with his hierarchy of needs model, and Douglas McGregor (1960), an admirer of Maslow, pointed out in his influential book, *The Human Side of Enterprise*, that in many parts of the world, human beings spontaneously participated in religious activities with gusto, but without any monetary incentives. Psychologists have long distinguished between extrinsic and intrinsic motivation, suggesting that humans are likely to be motivated by different factors, not money alone. Extrinsic factors other than money, such as validation or social approval, and intrinsic factors may begin to exert greater influence on human motivation.

Thus, human beings may still be responsive to incentives, but the character of those incentives would likely have changed.

Technology Policy

One of the remarkable feats of the 20th century is the rapid development of science and technology; in fact, it is this development that has enabled us even to contemplate the assumption of a workless society. This development has been the result of both individual entrepreneurial initiatives and government policies. Various governments have pursued somewhat differing policies, but it is also true that post-World War II, the US played a leading role in this development. The US had learned from the experiences of European countries, especially Germany, during the 19th century in industrial research, but has in turn contributed both to the conduct of research and the institutions that support research. Both of these — the conduct of research and institutions — may be disrupted by the arrival of a workless society.

Research, or knowledge creation, has typically been considered a non-routine task. Because of this characteristic, research could not be easily automated and has thus eluded the grasp of roboticization and digitalization. AI has been touted to automate *reasoning* process, the very heart of the research enterprise. If the claims about AI prove right, then the research enterprise is about to be disrupted.

A significant portion of research, perhaps the later stages of research, is conducted in for-profit organizations. It is likely that many of the research activities can be automated with the application of AI, with the early stages of this disruption taking the form of cost reduction. For example, AI is likely to create efficiencies in clinical trials where much of the research and development budget of big pharmaceutical companies is located. There is also evidence that AI will enable companies to identify product opportunities hitherto unforeseen.[2] Indeed, it is possible that what robotics did to the blue-collar workforce may be repeated among research

[2]There is evidence that AI has been applied to identify new products in many chemical companies.

personnel with AI. Evidence is also emerging that AI is being incorporated into basic research, although its pervasiveness and applicability are not yet known.[3] Thus, the prospect of worklessness is not confined to any specific sectors of society. In turn, this has profound implications for the structuring of the institutions we have built up in the past for research and development.

The US innovation system (Narayanan and O'Connor, 2010), perhaps the best developed in the world, has many critical features, but I will focus on three — the intellectual property laws, Bayh–Dole Act, and the cluster of government institutions like the National Science Foundation.

1. IP laws had been designed to promote scientific and artistic progress by balancing the incentives for innovation with the need for public access to information. They encourage investment in research and development, as inventors and creators can be confident that their intellectual property will be protected. They also help businesses compete in the marketplace by allowing them to distinguish their products and services from those of competitors.
2. The Bayh–Dole Act, a federal law enacted in 1980, enables universities, non-profit research institutions, and small businesses to own, patent, and commercialize inventions developed under federally funded research programs within their organizations.
3. Over the years, the US established a cluster of institutions to promote scientific progress, advance national health and prosperity, and secure national defense. For example, the National Science Foundation (NSF), established in 1950, supports basic research and education in all fields of science and engineering. NSF remains a major source of federal funding for research in fields like math, computer science, economics, and social sciences.

These and related institutional structures had been created to incentivize and fund knowledge creation and application activities. By all accounts, they had served the US admirably. However, in a workless society, both the incentives and funding may become irrelevant.

---

[3] See Chapter 6 on the US innovation system in the Encyclopedia of Technology and Innovation.

Yet identifying and channeling human creative potential will continue to be a significant challenge for which the current institutional structures may not be adequate. Indeed, many of these challenges may transcend national boundaries. For example, global climate change may need the participation of wide segments of the globe beyond the US boundaries. Similarly, space exploration may require collaborations across the world. Current institutional structures may, unfortunately, not be equipped to handle these challenges.

Sleepwalking to the Future

Marshall McLuhan[4] is reputed to have once said, "We look at the present through a rear-view mirror." That is, our past experiences and knowledge can blind us to the true implications of the present and future. Thus, when encountering new situations, especially those involving new technologies, people tend to interpret them through the lenses of the recent past. The technological developments and the possibility of a workless society that they have raised signal a qualitative break from the past. They invite fresh thinking rather than incremental changes in policies that are anchored in obsolete assumptions. In the previous chapter, I had illustrated the mortal grasp of obsolete assumptions in three policy domains. The past no longer supplies a realistic set of assumptions for us to build our collective future.

---

[4] The phrase, popularized by media theorist Marshall McLuhan, means that we tend to understand and react to new situations or technologies by applying frameworks and assumptions from the recent past. We "look at the present through a rear-view mirror" because, instead of grasping the present for what it is, we are constantly using the lens of past experiences and "marching backwards into the future". This can limit our understanding of new developments and cause us to miss their true potential.

Herbert Marshall McLuhan was a Canadian philosopher whose work is among the cornerstones of the study of media theory. He began his teaching career as a professor of English at several universities in the United States and Canada before moving to the University of Toronto in 1946, where he remained for the rest of his life. He is known as "the father of media studies". McLuhan coined the expression "the medium is the message" (in the first chapter of his *Understanding Media: The Extensions of Man*), as well as the term *global village*. He was a fixture in media discourse in the late 1960s, In the years following his death, he continued to be a controversial figure in academic circles. However, with the arrival of the Internet and the World Wide Web, interest was renewed in his work and perspectives.

Here, I simply enumerate three critical domains where policy discussions need to be focused and a national consensus forged.

Social control of technological development: There have been some discussions about the impact of technology on various facets in the US and Europe. In fact, Europe has taken some baby steps toward controlling the development of AI. None of these discussions adequately addresses the possibility of a workless society and the role of technology development in it. As I have attempted to show in the previous chapter, the policy debates are comfortably ensconced in industrial era assumptions and a scarcity mindset.

It is entirely acceptable that we as a society *reject* the notion of a workless society, just as in the Sci-fi, where nations decided to abandon computer technology. Alternatively, we may hasten the development of certain technologies that may end in a workless society. But what is problematic is the relegation of technology development to a group of technology elites, without a collective awareness of the developments' consequences for the many, and thus disenfranchising vast swaths of population on matters that will dictate their future.

Revisioning institutions: A workless society will certainly emasculate many of our institutions, ranging from our current conception of intellectual property, the nature of incentives, and the capacities required to foster technology development. Although many of our contemporary institutions have served us well and we owe a heavy debt of gratitude to the architects of these institutions for their vision and leadership, the institutions themselves reflect assumptions of an era that we can increasingly view in our rear-view mirror. Hence, it is time that we ask if many of these institutions are necessary for our purposes in the future unfolding in front of us. For example, if AI can do most of the activities involved in technology development, should we preserve institutional structures to incentivize individuals and organizations?

It is equally necessary that we confront the challenges of a workless society and ask if *new* institutions need to be built up to address both the leisure's discontents and the challenges that I had outlined in a previous chapter.

Rethinking our governance structures: Most importantly, technological developments leading to a workless society are fast outpacing the governance structures that we have built up over the years. The US has benefited enormously from its constitution, which a bunch of visionaries crafted over 200 years ago. The nation has also managed to fine-tune the constitution through a set of amendments that were needed to adapt it to the times and aspirations of the people. The constitution was crafted at a time when the world looked different, the country was still in transition to an industrial economy, and major wars had not been fought. It is unlikely that a strategy of incremental innovation through amendments is adequate for the seismic change that is thrust upon us by technology development. In the eighth chapter, I outlined at least three scenarios (excluding utopian structures) of probable governance structures, while acknowledging that this is only a selection of the possibilities. I suspect that to escape "McLuhan's" problem, we need to have a wider discussion of the kind of governance structures.

Essence of Being Human

As technological developments continue to strip away what had once been thought of as activities that require intervention by human beings, we are left to ponder the philosophical question of what it means to be human. Herbert Simon, a pioneer in the field of AI, once rattled the world of economics by challenging the rationality assumptions inherent in the then economic theory. His was an intellectual exercise and hence confined to the rarified domains of the academy. Ongoing technological developments are bringing the issue to the forefront of human awareness, and beyond the confines of the academy.

Descartes, a precursor to the Enlightenment, the great intellectual movement in Europe, is reputed to have once said, "Cogito ego sum." One interpretation of his now-famous statement is that we are human *because* we think. The Industrial Revolution only made it possible for machines to augment human physical capabilities, leaving reasoning skills alone. But digitalization and recent developments in AI have stripped the reasoning power of being a unique capability of humans.

So then, what is unique about us, humans? A workless society will create a context in which human reasoning capabilities, even in specific domains, would not be the basis for defining our identities. Thus, we are entering a *regenerative* period in our history when we will have to rethink some enduring but fundamental questions: Who are we? How should we organize our societies? To answer these questions, we will require leadership at the global level, a topic I touch upon to close the book.

A Call for Leadership

Technological developments and the ensuing possibility of a workless society have thus raised existential questions about human identity, our cultures, and governance structures. Should we develop 'super' humans through neurobiology? Should we control technology development itself to fulfill our goals or let technology develop autonomously? How should we recreate our governance structures to meet the moment?

Questions such as these require lenses broader than technological for answers. Indeed, these questions will require collective processes to debate and discuss our varying viewpoints. This process will have to engage our least informed, our weakest, and our poorest; only then are they likely to succeed, without devolving into revolutions. Thus, we are at a generative period in time, faced with a unique opportunity to control our own evolution. Although we may not yet see the rainbow, getting 'there' will require enlightened leadership. The construction of the US Constitution, where a few creative individuals navigated through a difficult process, is one example from history. We may have to replicate their accomplishments, but perhaps do better than them because our context is different and more complex. Challenges of a workless society depend on such leaders for resolution.

References

MacGregor, D. (1960). *The Human Side of Enterprise*, 21(166). New York: McGraw-Hill.

Narayanan, V. K. and O'Connor, G. C. (eds.). (2010). *Encyclopedia of technology and innovation management*. John Wiley & Sons.

Index

www.ingramcontent.com/pod-product-compliance
Ingram Content Group UK Ltd.
Pitfield, Milton Keynes, MK11 3LW, UK
UKHW061000120926
8556IPUK00032B/891

9 789819 827749